THE NEW PRECIOUS METALS MARKET

How the Changes in
Fundamentals Are Creating
Extraordinary Profit Opportunities

PHILIP GOTTHELF

McGraw-Hill

New York San Francisco Washington, D.C. Auckland Bogotá
Caracas Lisbon London Madrid Mexico City Milan
Montreal New Delhi San Juan Singapore
Sydney Tokyo Toronto

Library of Congress Cataloging-in-Publication Data

Author: Gotthelf, Philip.
Title: The new precious metals market: How changes in the fundamentals
                 are creating extraordinary profit opportunities /
                 Philip Gotthelf.
Published: New York : McGraw-Hill, 1998.
Description: p. cm.
LC Call No.:   HG261.G68 1998
Dewey No.:   332.63 21
ISBN: 0786308400
Subjects: Precious metals—United States.
                 Investment analysis.
                 Metals as an investment—United States.
                 Securities—United States.
Control No.:   97035304

McGraw-Hill

A Division of The McGraw-Hill Companies

  2 3 4 5 6 7 8 9 0 DOC/DOC 9 0 2 1 0 9 8

ISBN 0-7863-0840-0

The sponsoring editor for this book was *Stephen Isaacs*, the editing supervisor was *John M. Morriss*, and the production supervisor was *Suzanne W. B. Rapcavage*. It was set in Palatino by *Judy Brown*.

Printed and bound by R. R. Donnelley & Sons Company.

McGraw-Hill books are available at special quantity discounts to use as premiums and sales promotions, or for use in corporate training programs. For more information, please write to the Director of Special Sales, McGraw-Hill, 11 West 19th Street, New York, NY 10011. Or contact your local bookstore.

 This book is printed on recycled, acid-free paper containing a minimum of 50% recycled de-inked fiber.

CONTENTS

ACKNOWLEDGMENTS

John M. Ball, Director of Trading, EQUIDEX Brokerage Group, Inc.

The COMEX Division of the New York Mercantile Exchange

The Entire Staff of EQUIDEX

Johnson Matthey PLC and Johnson Matthey North America

Paula Gotthelf, Editing and Research Assistant

Robert Hafer, Bridge Data

United States Mint, Washington, D.C.

SOURCES

The Gold Institute, 1112 Sixteenth Street, N.W., Suite 240, Washington, D.C. 20036, U.S.A.

The World Gold Council, 900 Third Avenue, New York, New York 10022, U.S.A.; 1 Rue de la Rotisserie, CH-1204 Geneva, Switzerland.

The United States Bureau of Mines, Denver, Colorado.

MacKay School of Mines, University of Nevada, Reno, Nevada.

Gold Fields Mineral Services Ltd., Greencoat House, Francis Street, London SW1P 1DH, U.K.

Commodity Yearbook, Bridge (formerly Knight-Ridder Financial), 30 South Wacker Drive, Chicago, Illinois 60606-7404.

CRB INFOTECH® CD-ROM, Bridge Data.

Moore Research Center, 321 West 13th Avenue, Eugene, Oregon 97401.

ASSOCIATIONS

Alaska Miners Association
American Institute of Mining
Australian Institute of Geoscientists
British Columbia & Yukon Chamber of Mines
Canadian Geotechnical Society
Geological Association of Canada
The Geological Survey of Japan
The Minerals, Metals & Materials Society

JOURNALS AND PUBLICATIONS

California Mining Journal
Hard Rock Analyst
Journal of Electronic Materials
Metal Bulletin
Mining Journal
The New York Times
The Wall Street Journal

INTRODUCTION

Not long ago, gold and silver played primary monetary roles. From about the mid-nineteenth century through 1975, these metals were used to regulate global money supplies. Humanity has placed faith and trust in noble metals for thousands of years. Through the ages, we have exchanged goods and services for pieces of silver and judged the wealth of kings in terms of gold. Even when we became sophisticated enough to realize paper was easier to handle than coin, we continued to "back currency" with metal. Yet, after years of loyal service as our means of exchange, gold and silver fell from grace within a decade. From 1975, when gold became a legal asset for U.S. citizens to possess, through 1985, when prices failed to recover from a spectacular rise and fall, precious metals in general lost their investment luster.

In the 1990s, venerable newspapers dropped gold as an economic indicator. Silver was reduced to "just a commodity." The degree to which the world turned its back on these metals astounded those who lived through the first half of the twentieth century. At the same time, paper assets created unprecedented wealth. From surging fixed-income returns occurring during the 1980s to a raging bull equities market in the 1990s, paper truly became king while traditional stores of value like hard assets and real estate proved unworthy of consideration. A friend asked, "Why write about precious metals if their investment role is lost? What purpose is a review if new financial vehicles and strategies have taken over?" Perhaps we need a well-founded explanation for the lack of investment performance of silver and gold from 1980 through 1997. Facts are clouded by emotional interpretations and self-serving reports. Consider that during the gold and silver price declines of the 1980s, "gold bugs" insisted a bull market was just around the corner. Little negative news came from industry groups. In the face of static performance, gold and silver received constant promotion to the point of crying wolf. Despite a steady rise in production, we heard the world constantly faced a "shortage"—exactly what die-hard bulls wanted us to believe.

Reality painted a different picture. In the aftermath of the 1980 peaks, metals yielded to surging interest rates and a massive anti-inflation effort. Suddenly, interest rates offered returns well in excess of inflation. Passive strategies like buying and holding bonds proved surprisingly profitable. At the same time, mining capacity was building rather than shrinking. Demand for base metals translated into secondary silver and gold production. Platinum recovery and refinement etched away at a rising demand curve. Effectively, supply was meeting demand. The move away from precious metals was a wise decision. The paper chase was on.

WHAT TARNISHED PRECIOUS METALS?

To truly understand the plight of precious metals, it is important to explore fundamental supply and demand changes that drove prices to unthinkable lows in the face of continuing inflation. For anyone evaluating precious metals, a clear view of events from 1980 through 1997 lays a foundation for successful investing in the future. Yes, gold and silver are vulnerable to progress and changing investment moods. No, gold and silver are not always the most appropriate vehicles for investment funds. So, this text addresses these issues as objectively as possible.

With such a perspective, a new age of precious metals investing in a new market has emerged that also requires explanation. Technology is changing the way we mine and use precious metals. In fact, the entire precious metals market structure has been changing. Fundamentals related to supply and demand are different. Monetary systems are different. Political systems have changed. There are new investment vehicles. Strategies must be redefined. These are reasons for a book about modern precious metals investing. The chapters ahead explore traditional roles of silver, gold, and industrial precious metals like platinum and palladium. The text takes a broad and comprehensive view of supply and demand, answering the critical question, "Should you invest or speculate in precious metals?" If so, what are the best ways?

Acceptance of a Floating Exchange

From 1980 through the first half of the 1990s, I was an outspoken precious metals bear. On the NBC "Today Show," I predicted silver would fall from $6.50 an ounce in 1988 to less than $4.00 over the next several years. In the face of one inflation prediction after another, I held fast to my belief that silver would not regain its footing and gold would not manage a long-awaited rally. Reasons were simple. An objective look at supply patterns revealed increasing production with static consumption. This logic did not stand alone. In addition to expanding supplies, gold and silver "decoupled" with currency parity. In other words, currency was no longer compared with gold or silver to derive a relative value against other currencies. The global monetary system had confidence in a floating exchange that could be easily traded like commodities.

When viewed as "commodities," currencies fluctuated in accordance with their own supply and demand forces. If the German mark was gaining strength against the U.S. dollar, traders could move from dollars into deutsche marks. Where was gold? Who needed gold? Periods of inflation proved selective and regional. Thus, investors could maneuver from an inflating currency into more stable paper. In the "old days," gold and silver could be used to offset effects of rising and falling interest rates. However, in the early 1980s, new markets like Ginnie Mae futures, T-bond futures, interest rate options, and a host of other "derivative" vehicles diminished requirements for hard asset hedges. In a rising interest rate environment, traders could sell interest rate derivatives like futures and options. As rates retreated, futures and options could be purchased. Simply put, gold and silver were displaced through financial invention.

Technology

In the wings, rapid information dissemination and processing also took a toll on gold and silver. Traditional behavior dictated moving into metals when uncertainty needed to be sorted out. While investors waited for facts and interpretations, gold and silver were comfortable places to store wealth. When the Information Age exploded, the "uncertainty hedge" dissipated. We had facts faster. We could analyze impact more easily. If there are any doubts about the influence of information processing on investment markets, correlate the decline in silver and gold with the rise of the personal computer. Consider that new derivative financial vehicles would not be possible if computers were not available to rapidly and accurately calculate values and extrapolate relationships.

In my earlier book entitled *Techno Fundamental Trading*, I touched on "synthetic investing." That book was published in 1995. Within a year, synthetic investing had expanded into "cyber investing." Investments could be created from information. An index could become a contract. A contract could be exchanged. It could all take place on the Internet in cyber markets—paid for with cyber money in cyber transactions. It seemed the status of gold and silver would continue to deteriorate. After all, you could bring up a pretty good picture of precious metals on a Web site. Perhaps we can even have the sensation of touching, holding, or wearing gold in "virtual reality." Who needs the real thing?

Responding to this move into cyberspace, I now caution that instability is inherent in the system. A data glitch or program failure can bring cyber markets crashing down. One thing is certain: gold and silver are real; virtual reality isn't. As we move away from reality, will we need reality? At what point will we question the validity of cyber cash or even dollar bills? As technology races forward, it will be easier to produce $100 bills complete with embedded coding strips on a high-resolution color printer. Forged holograph imprints will be no problem. What's real? Who will know for sure? Your credit cards, voice, fingerprints—everything used for transactions—will be vulnerable to technological tampering in the wrong hands. Where will we place our trust as technology advances? Perhaps we will be forced to return to our old standards. As one Generation Xer said, "Gold's cool."

THE BASICS OF PRECIOUS METALS

Although examining new market developments is intriguing, a text on precious metals investing is not complete without reviewing basics. Yes, cyberspace is fascinating, but what are gold, silver, platinum, and palladium, and where do these metals come from? How are they used? Why are they valuable? Do we consume silver, platinum, and palladium as opposed to gold? What technologies will expand or contract precious metal consumption? How might computers replace platinum as a means for cleaning engine emissions? Will new engines eliminate the need for catalytic converters? How much platinum do we use each year for these catalytic converters? The basics are important if we are to profit from precious metals in the years ahead.

As rapidly as technology is advancing, so is political change. Again, we can thank information technology for much of the "globalization" process that has torn down barriers and constructed new political incentives that can drive precious metals. Consider that the majority of the gold and silver hoard is stored in central bank vaults. These metals remain political assets. If there has truly been a divorce between money and the sibling metals, someone forgot to inform central banks. In fact, treasuries are not too keen on the idea of selling precious metal inventories, a process referred to as *divestment*. What is the significance of global gold reserves? What are the important influences gold reserves have upon investment strategies? Alone, explorations of silver and gold politics can fill several books.

To appreciate the big picture, this book explores geology, mining, refining, and applications of these metals. How do copper prices affect silver, gold, platinum, and palladium? What about other base metals like nickel, tin, zinc, lead, and iron? Can fusion and fission technology dictate precious metal prices? What about religion, population, demographics, and education? Can we be conditioned to abandon gold and silver? Can we be taught that these are simply metals like all others? Is there a "master plan"?

Finally, the book considers strategies. How can you invest in precious metals? Why should you invest? When should you invest? Are stocks better than physical metal? What about futures and options? Should you consider rare coins, medallions, and coin of the realm? What is the significance of face value?

Does it all sound interesting and exciting? Let's get started!

CHAPTER 1

What's All the Fuss About?

THE LURE OF PRECIOUS METALS

Gold

See it. Hold it. Move it from hand to hand and bring it up to the light. If you have ever seen and held an ingot of pure 24-karat gold you know it is not "just a commodity." There is something fascinating about this metal. I believe it truly has mystical powers over human emotions. When I was twelve years old, I visited the Federal Reserve vault in New York City to see the "backing" for the U.S. currency. Gold and silver were still linked to the money supply. It was illegal for private U.S. citizens to own bulk quantities of gold. There it was. Bricks of gold lay before me in absolute glowing splendor. I was excited. I was moved! After all, I was raised on stories of pirates and treasure rather than Bevis and Butthead. My father told me about spending gold. He gave me a $5 gold piece just before my visit to the vault. Gosh, it was fun. I'll never forget it. Perhaps that is why gold has held a unique place in the hearts and minds of men and women. It's just great!

Years after my visit to the New York Federal Reserve, I was invited into the vault of a private bullion dealer. It was just after the U.S. gold prohibition had been lifted in 1975. Although the quantity I saw there was not as impressive as that in the New York Federal Reserve, I was invited to lift the pure ingots. Some readers will understand when I say the weight-to-size ratio is astounding. We all may know gold is one of Earth's heaviest elements. Yet, to lift a gold brick with a grunt or feel a hand-sized ingot that weighs a kilo is totally unexpected, enlightening, and exhilarating. There is simply nothing like it. No matter how unemotional you may want to be toward this metal, a personal encounter with gold in bulk is a profound experience for most of us.

Virtually every society holds gold as a symbol of value. Whether it has been "demonetized" by governments and central banks or is "remonetized," gold maintains a parity relationship with all the world's currencies. Simply put, gold is a fact of human existence and I doubt we will ever mature to the point where we all consider it "just a commodity."

From the time I had my personal encounter to the hours I spent writing this book, I have always enjoyed my gold craving. This is not to say that I am a "gold bug." In fact, from 1980 through the publication of this book, I was more of a bear than a bull. Still, the craving persisted. I love to see and feel pure gold ingots. It's delightful. It's fascinating. It is awe-inspiring. The effect gold has on people is its very salvation. Reality suggests that gold has very little usefulness beyond its perceived value. Industrial demand is fractional in relation to investment demand. It is said that most of the gold mined throughout history is accounted for today. Gold is not consumed. It is stored and sometimes worshipped.

Silver

Turn your attention to silver. Although silver is less mouth watering to some, you need only see a proof-struck coin to understand how silver rose to reverence. With its mirror complexion and white sparkle, silver represents the perfect complement to gold. Together, silver and gold form a complete picture. If you don't believe me, make an effort to view polished gold and silver side by side. I doubt you could honestly say you had absolutely no urge to own a bit of each.

From my first birthday through my teens, I had an uncle who sent me one silver dollar for each year of my age—one for my first year, two for my second, and so on. Every so often, I would go into my closet and take out the thick cotton bag with a reddish brown drawstring that safely held my silver stash. Although it was hardly appropriate treatment for the venerable coins, I enjoyed clinking them into a small pile. (I admit that I polished one even after being told it would adversely affect its value.) Like gold, silver has an innate appeal. Maybe this is because of its reflective properties. Perhaps it is the ring when a silver coin is dropped just right. It is a lustrous metal that beautifully applies to eating and serving utensils, jewelry, mirrors, and ornaments.

At dawn, the sky lights up with a fiery golden hue. In the evening, the moon reflects a silvery pattern on an ocean, a lake, or a bay. Gold and silver are the most inspiring colors in nature. If you disagree, examine our literature. Study the history. Nothing on earth short of life itself has been more revered than gold or silver. That's what the fuss is about.

Platinum

Of course, the family is not really complete. Platinum joins silver and gold with its appealing bright and deep silvery shine. The weight and uncanny hardness add to the attraction. This is a difficult metal to refine. It is relatively new in our history, yet it has made remarkable inroads as a supreme value. Platinum has character all to itself. As we will examine, this metal along with its sisters palladium and rhodium can claim unique chemical properties. Unlike gold, with its stability and noble physical properties, the "platinum group" is reactive. Platinum's tight molecular lattice provides catalytic capabilities for small molecule compounds like hydrocarbons. Platinum is a valuable industrial commodity with vast applications and irreplaceable functions. There is an important role for platinum in any precious metals investment strategy.

Palladium

The trio of gold, silver, and platinum represents the "precious metals group" for most people. However, this is still not a total picture. Palladium has enjoyed widening popularity. Until 1989, palladium remained relatively obscure. Its first real public appearance came with the announcement of cold fusion by two University of Utah professors in March of that year. Palladium was hailed as the potential source of clean, cheap, limitless energy. Prices surged from less than $100 to more than $180 per ounce. When cold fusion was condemned as fraud and folly by the scientific community, palladium prices promptly plunged to a low below $78 per ounce. However, an impression was made.

Interest in palladium for cold fusion continued and may eventually result in commercially feasible processes that this book reviews later in greater detail. In the aftermath of the initial cold fusion fiasco, palladium gained other respectability as a substitute for platinum in automotive and truck catalytic converters. Palladium also gathered momentum in electronic components, dental alloys, and chemical processes.

Rhodium

Are you familiar with rhodium? With the exception of exotic and forbidden metals like purified uranium and plutonium, rhodium has held some of the most spectacular values per ounce of any precious metal. Rhodium saw prices above $7,000 per ounce in the 1980s. It is vital for certain processing technology and is essential in the three-way catalytic converter. When you consider a metal that can vary more than $4,000 an ounce, you are looking at the ultimate speculative precious metal—as of 1995.

Unfortunately, as of this writing, rhodium can be traded only as a cash commodity. There are no futures contracts or exchange-traded options for rhodium. This dearth means investors cannot use leverage to participate in rhodium trading. In addition, it is difficult to buy rhodium if you are not a dealer or user. In short, rhodium is not an easy investment.

ORIGINS OF PRECIOUS METALS

In addition to examining precious metals investing, it is helpful to understand the metals themselves. What is gold? Where did it come from? Is there some cosmic reason why it is so rare and so interesting? Similar questions apply to silver, platinum, and palladium. To appreciate their place in our universe, we must go back in time to the very beginning of matter. Most of us are aware of the Big Bang Theory. It postulates that our universe and all within it formed in a huge cosmic explosion billions of years ago. Obviously, this massive event involved enormous heat and energy that we are just beginning to comprehend through advanced nuclear physics. In reality, we have very little understanding about the origins of matter. The world's greatest minds are still pondering the forces that bind the universe together. Scientists continue searching for a universal theory that explains how and why the cosmos in its entirety functions. You may hear about new Unified Field theories and Perfect Symmetry. Eventually, someone will get it right. However, this book focuses on the formation of the elemental chain or periodic table, which is reasonably established through observation.

The first element was hydrogen, the building block of all elements and first on the periodic table with an atomic weight of 1.008. Hydrogen is the primary fuel of the galaxies. It is believed that huge hydrogen clouds condensed under gravity in the early universe. As these massive clouds contracted, enormous pressures began building until hydrogen began to fuse into helium. This process powers most visible stars.

Stellar fusion does not end there. Throughout billions of years, all of a star's hydrogen is eventually fused into helium. Because helium is a denser element, greater forces build up that cause helium to fuse into lithium. As elemental fusion climbs up the periodic table, a star implodes to the point where forces cause an explosion or a black hole. If a star explodes into a nova or supernova, there is a chance it will be reborn.

This is believed to be the process that formed our own sun. The debris or "stardust" is thought to be the origin of planets. In effect, everything in our physical world is stardust. It stands to reason that the higher the element is on the periodic table, the later its evolution in the fusion process. In addition, it seems logical that the fusion process in higher elements did not last as long as primary reactions. Thus, many higher elements on the table are also more rare. As a percentage of matter in the universe, gold and the platinum group are among the smallest. Not only are these metals rare on earth, it is reasonable to assume they are rare throughout existence. Having established this fact, we might conclude that precious metals truly have a universal appeal if scarcity is a primordial determinant of value. Not only would humankind value these metals, so might any other civilizations sprinkled throughout the universe.

WHY PRECIOUS METALS ARE PRECIOUS

Of course, the positions of precious metals on the periodic table are not their only basis for value. Virtually all precious metals exhibit extraordinary properties that establish value based on function. Moreover, from an earthly viewpoint, gold, silver, and the platinum group are uniquely deposited throughout the globe. Mining and refining processes are difficult. Discovery is tedious. Recovery is expensive. All of this adds to the allure of precious metals. As later chapters explain, each metal has a vital industrial or monetary role. Eventually, technology or invention can displace usage.

By the same token, technology or invention can create new roles and applications. There are strong indications that precious metals may account for political and monetary power at some point in the future. Control over these metals may represent control over government and society. I can assure even the most skeptical reader that my personal love affair with precious metals is shared by most of the population. The psychological attraction binding us to precious metals defines their primary role. Ownership is a sign of power. Power is a means to dominate. For now, humans are an aggressive species. This implies that power and dominance will continue as our motivation throughout the twenty-first century and beyond. If gold, silver, and platinum group metals gain monetary or industrial significance, those who own will be those who lead. This is what the fuss is about.

If you are a citizen of the industrialized West, your perspective is probably much different from that of a citizen of the Far East, Middle East, or India. Throughout most cultures, gold is as much a symbol as a monetary standard. Consider the simple wedding band: a symbol of love, dedication, and a contract between husband and wife. The ring may weigh only a few grams and have a purity of less than 14 karats. Yet when multiplied by the number of married couples, these small items can amount to robust annual demand that expands with the overall population. More importantly, from 1972 forward, liquidity and wealth began more rapid expansion in regions where a wedding can call for as much as a kilo of gold among even lower classes.

As later chapters detail, liquidity, population, and tradition are likely to dictate the next major gold trends. This will be extremely important as investors decide which precious metals offer speculative opportunities. Only gold carries the extensive ritualistic significance that can define demand.

To a lesser extent, silver can perk up as weddings increase. We are all familiar with grandma's silver service. Unfortunately, convenience and the fast pace of modern living have tarnished the tradition of "bringing out the silver." Few within the general population have the time or inclination to set a proper table, let alone polish the silver. It is possible for tradition to come full circle. At some point, we may return to elegant and formal dining with appropriate sterling silver settings. However, the current trend points to a declining number of brides registering for silver services. Thus, it is unlikely silver can count on an increase in global population to the same extent as gold. Some may argue that silver's future lies in its primary industrial application: photography. As global populations become more sophisticated and wealthy, demand for photographic records will grow. More importantly, we should see a steady rise in demand for professional photography, X-ray, and photolithographic printing. Travel, a new baby boom, emerging newspapers and magazines, upgraded health care . . . the list of positive factors for silver goes on and on.

Of course, not every cloud has its silver lining. Technology, which gave silver its industrial life, could soon take a toll on the "white metal." Computer imaging and digital photography loom on the horizon as the greatest threat to as much as 30 percent of all annual silver production.

It is interesting that precious metals are among the least understood "investments." Perhaps this is because few people are aware of historical roles for these elements. Even the most sophisticated investors harbor a distorted view of how gold and silver have been used over the centuries. Essentially, the view of precious metals has been clouded by all the fuss. Is it surprising to learn that gold and silver have played very brief roles as monetary instruments? Is it shocking to find that precious metals have not performed well as long-term investments? Is it unimaginable to discover that precious metals are among the weakest "hard-asset" performers?

Understand that much of the modern-day fuss about precious metals was spawned by only two events. First was the Gold Rush that began in the western United States in 1849. This was the first inspiration for a dramatic increase in gold supply since the discovery and early exploitation of the New World. Although many Americans narrowly believe the Gold Rush was limited to the United States, those with a more general knowledge are aware that the event circled the globe and lasted through 1920. (In fact, there is a Gold Rush today.)

The second great event was the post-Energy Crisis inflation of the 1970s that pushed precious metals to unthinkable heights and threatened to unravel our trust in the global monetary system. Silver approached $50 an ounce (Figure 1–1). Gold reached levels above $800 (Figure 1–2). Platinum soared to $1,000 an ounce (Figure 1–3) and palladium blasted beyond $400 (Figure 1–4). These were truly spectacular price movements that occurred from 1978 through 1980. As "speculative" vehicles, precious metals had no match. It seems this single event left an indelible impression

F I G U R E 1–1

Silver made its most memorable move of the twentieth century during 1979–1980. Inflation fears and a speculative scheme by the Hunt brothers drove prices to spectacular levels.

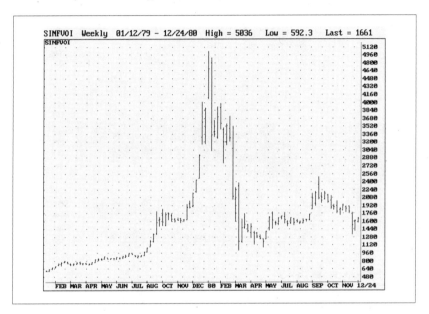

among investors and converted gold, silver, platinum, and palladium into would-be investments.

Many may argue that this book should emphasize major events like the use of metal to back currency. They might claim that this book should consider the gold realignment of the U.S. dollar by President Roosevelt. What about the confiscation of gold from U.S. citizens? American history features the Bretton Woods Agreement and Nixon's closing of the U.S. gold window. Obviously, there are many important developments in the history of precious metals. Although the book may touch on these events, a complete historical perspective is beyond the scope and goal of this text.

F I G U R E   1–2

Gold followed silver in what has been labeled the "go-go years" for precious metals.

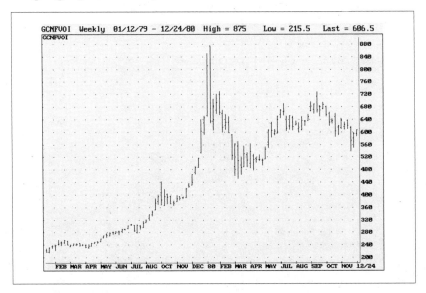

F I G U R E   1–3

Platinum followed gold and silver in tandem.

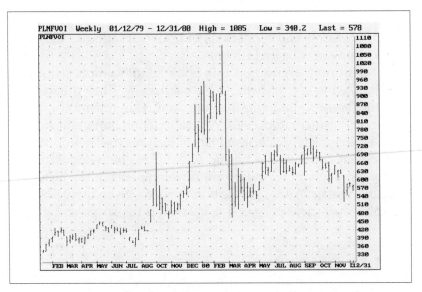

F I G U R E 1–4

Perhaps the most impressive showing was
palladium, which moved from less than $90 to $410
in the cash market.

HOW PRECIOUS METALS WILL REMAIN PRECIOUS

Rather than simply recap history, it is essential to understand
traditional roles and traditional market structures. Obviously,
gold and silver have played significant monetary and political
roles. Platinum and palladium have not. The key to understanding the new nature of precious metals markets is to evaluate
whether traditional roles can return or if new roles will emerge.
Will people ever carry gold or silver coins again? Will central
banks ever return to a monetary standard based upon silver or
gold values? Is the real opportunity in industrial applications like
platinum fuel cells, silver-based computer memory cards, gold
plasma "sono-luminescence" reactors, or superconductive alloys?
In other words, it may be time to turn our attention away from
tradition toward the new and different. The future of these markets and associated speculative opportunities depends on such an
altered perspective.

Perhaps a historical overview tells us we will always have a special interest in precious metals. That may be the extent of what we can learn from the past. Our history in its entirety has been brief. Consider that if four generations span each century, recorded history covers fewer than 400 generations. People may be surprised to discover that much of what they believe about silver and gold is myth. Yes, gold has been worshipped for centuries but infrequently used as money. Copper and silver have been vehicles for exchange. Patterns and trends suggest this may continue to be true in the future. Major events can cause a "revolution" in precious metals as well as an "evolution."

CHAPTER 2

Monetary Roles

Metals have been directly used as money. Certainly, we are familiar with copper, silver, and gold coins. This has been the most basic use as monetary instruments. As economic systems evolved in the nineteenth century, silver and gold were linked as monetary standards and coupled with currency. These actions established two-tiered monetary systems and were responsible for rapid economic expansion during the Industrial Revolution. This evolution of world economies was the direct result of several gold discoveries, including the U.S. Gold Rush beginning in 1849. Believe it or not, the gold rush continues today.

LINKING MONEY WITH METALS

Prior to the huge expansion in gold production, monetary linkage primarily focused on more plentiful silver and other coinage. This is an important consideration because effective monetary linkage depends on plentiful supplies. The lack of sufficient gold from the 1960s through 1975 and a lack of ownership diversity were the most significant reasons gold was abandoned as a global monetary standard.

Limitations of Using Gold Reserves

The period following World War I mobilized industries. The expansion that followed came to an abrupt end with the stock market crash of 1929. Although excessive speculation was a catalyst for the meltdown, a liquidity crisis plunged the United States and companion nations into depression. The ultimate solution was to increase the U.S. money supply by raising the official price of gold from $20.67 to $35 an ounce in 1934. To promote monetary stability among industrialized nations, the U.S. Treasury agreed to buy and sell gold for monetary purposes at the official price. Thus, the dollar was linked to gold and other currencies could be linked to the dollar. This in turn led to the Bretton Woods Agreement that allowed member currencies to be narrowly adjusted around the gold/dollar standard. The international monetary system based on Bretton Woods existed from 1946 to 1971. However, the limitations of using gold as the official "reserve asset" became apparent as countries developed trade dislocations with deficits and surpluses.

In particular, postwar Germany took advantage of its ability to focus on consumer industries without the need for extensive military expenditures. Having lost the war, Germany was denied an internal military industrial complex for its own use. This freed economic resources (capital and labor) to build strong export industries. The result was an inflow of dollars and an outflow of goods. Germany took advantage of the U.S. Gold Window, which permitted the exchange of dollars for gold at the official price, by turning in dollars for gold. Other nations took similar action on a lesser scale. By 1960, the United States faced a run on its gold reserves. The London gold fix jumped to $40 and there was an automatic incentive to convert dollars at $35 per ounce into gold at $40. Although countries wanted to place their faith in a gold-backed U.S. dollar, it appears obvious that holding the metal was preferable.

This brings up an important consideration. When precious metals are freely traded, there is an automatic arbitrage created by official pricing or assigning face value. For example, if silver is selling for $1 an ounce on the free market, the government can buy at $1 and coin the metal at $5. There is an automatic gain of $4 on the transaction. However, if silver moves to $10, an investor can buy the coin from the government at $5 and sell in the free market for a profit. Further, if production is in private hands and unrestricted, there is no incentive to sell to the government unless payment is at the market price. Official pricing has a similar effect when the system has convertibility.

Investments versus Monetary Vehicles

During the 1980s and 1990s, governments have issued "coin of the realm." The $5 silver Maple Leaf of Canada and the silver U.S. dollar are examples of "investment coinage." Because these coins have face value, the presumption is that buyers have a floor under which the parity value cannot decline. Traditionally, governments have not marked up values to earn profits based on face value. When silver moved below $5 an ounce in the 1990s, collectors had the comfort of knowing they could use their coins as money. In effect, face value *did* preserve a portion of their investment.

Often, we fail to realize that when metals are used as monetary vehicles, investment value approaches zero. This is because relative value is established by caveat rather than market forces. Consider that a potential consequence of moving to a gold or silver standard can be the official confiscation of metals from private owners. Assuredly, the owner would not receive the ultimate value for gold or silver if such an event were to take place. There is no growth potential because value is fixed. Thus, if the United States were to return to a "gold standard," it is unlikely that physical gold would hold any appreciation potential. This does not mean that gold cannot provide safety during a monetary crisis. In the long run, any time there is monetary linkage, speculation becomes difficult or impossible. In the short run, owning gold or silver can offset the possibility of suffering from a "monetary realignment."

In a single-tier system, commodities are directly related to a single form of money. For silver, the unit may be the troy ounce.

Economic forces determine how much "parity" an ounce of silver will have with various goods and services. A pound of grain might be associated with an ounce of silver. If a pound of grain is considered half as valuable as a pound of beef, then two ounces of silver would be required to buy a pound of beef. All values for goods and services evolve from cross parity against the standard like an ounce of silver. Parity is simply a ratio between commodities or money. The alternative is to use barter, whereby two pounds of grain would be exchanged for one pound of beef. Obviously, using cross parity against a monetary standard is more effective.

The purpose of moving from barter to money was to allow the easy exchange of diverse goods and services. Because silver was far more plentiful than gold, it was the common precious metal used for money. By comparison, gold was so rare that it was used for ornaments more than as money. Gold coins minted before the Common Era were more commemorative than monetary. This is because it was impractical to create units of gold small enough for everyday transactions. A monetary standard needs certain long-range characteristics to survive. Quantity is a primary consideration.

Linking Metals with Economic Systems

Generally, survival in a single-tier system requires the money supply to grow at the same pace as the economy. As the population increases, so will demand for goods and services. If the money supply remains constant, goods and services will "deflate" relative to the standard. At some stage, the money supply may dwindle to the point where the system no longer functions. Scarce money often results in economic depressions. When the general population or governments cannot obtain enough of the existing money, a new form is likely to emerge.

Two developments significantly changed the global pace of economic expansion. First was the Age of Mercantilism, which converted economic systems from feudalism and localized structure to more global and trade-based economies. The wealth of nations was not simply based upon internal resources, but also the ability to trade. Mercantilism greatly enhanced the availability of goods and the need for monetary standards. International trade required international monetary standards. Gold and silver satisfied the requirement.

Following the Age of Mercantilism the world entered the Industrial Revolution, which in turn led to the New Age of Transportation. In some respects, the Age of Transportation began with Mercantilism because it flowed from shipping. Once railroads were developed the world had a truly complementary trade system. However, the real significance of the Industrial Age was its impact upon economic growth and technological innovation. Entirely new industries were born that demanded more money to support more wages, raw material purchases, plant and equipment investment, and expanding trade. As if to answer economic prayers, gold was discovered at Sutter's Mill in California to usher in the 1849 Gold Rush. It has been estimated that more gold was mined and processed between 1800 and 1900 than in the previous fifty centuries. This rapid expansion of an internationally recognized monetary standard fueled industrialization.

It is interesting to note that gold was a significant monetary standard for only two centuries. In the beginning of the eighteenth century, Sir Isaac Newton "fixed" the price of gold to the pound when he was master of the mint. However, more formal currency linkages were not established until the middle of the nineteenth century. In effect, gold's reign as primary standard was limited to the approximately eighty years extending from 1850 through 1930, excluding the suspension during World War I. The Great Depression proved the limitation of a fixed standard when the world's post-World War I economy ran into a monetary wall. Consider that the solution to the Depression was a revaluation of gold, which allowed the United States to expand its money supply. This was the first hint that gold could no longer sustain its role as the international monetary standard in the modern era.

When a two-tiered system was developed, silver and gold coins circulated along with redeemable certificates. In the United States, individual bank scrip that was redeemable in gold gave way to federal notes that could also be exchanged for gold. Franklin D. Roosevelt foreclosed gold redemption and ownership, and the basic U.S. economy returned to silver coinage. Great Britain had taken such a step two years earlier. International debts were still settled in gold; however, the public carried silver in their pockets and only silver certificates were honored in the United States. Even silver gave way to "full faith and credit" in the 1950s as supply pressures limited the ability to freely circulate silver as money. During the two-tiered system of exchange, paper assumed its value from its gold and silver parity. Gold's value was fixed to silver, which was fixed to a unit of exchange like the U.S. dollar or the British pound. This is not to be confused with bimetalic systems, which can be either single-tier or two-tier. Understand that the first tier is the metal whereas the second tier is the paper. Using two metals like gold and silver allows more paper or more coin to be issued. The restriction comes when one metal outstrips the other by becoming disproportionately more valuable.

Money is a means for transacting business. Money represents value. Money drives economies. Some economists believe money should be stable. Usually, money is earned. Sometimes, money is found. Circumstances surrounding the Gold Rush promoted a "get-rich-quick" mentality. Thousands of prospectors flocked to alleged gold fields seeking the Mother Lode. Some were lucky; most were not. Yet, gold fever left an almost indelible feeling that gold was the universal key to wealth. If you could find gold, you would be rich. This logic holds even as we move toward the twenty-first century. Despite the divorce between gold and money, there is still a huge effort to discover new ore deposits.

Silver glistened almost as much as gold following the inflationary 1970s. Early in that decade, a series of shortages ignited a global price spiral. First, weather patterns caused a crop failure in the Soviet Union that followed on the heels of a devastating 1971 corn blight in the United States. Back-to-back with these events, a warming of Pacific Ocean currents off the west coast of South America destroyed the Peruvian fish meal harvest. This important source of animal feed placed significant pressure upon grain prices. The famous Russian Wheat Deal of 1972–73 drove world prices for wheat, corn, and soybeans to record highs. Food prices significantly inflated. Thereafter, Middle Eastern oil producers banned together to embargo exports to the United States in retaliation for supporting Israel. Energy prices skyrocketed. These events culminated in an upward price spiral that challenged the public's confidence in money by the end of that decade. One extremely powerful oil family in the United States, the Hunts, attempted to resurrect a silver monetary standard while cornering the silver market. They almost succeeded.

In the wake of a fantastic upward price trend, investors flocked to silver. Everything from silver bullion to bags of old silver coins became popular investments. People sold grandma's silverware. Silver futures became the hottest game in town. But, as quickly as the silver bonanza exploded, it fizzled. A concerted effort to break the Hunts' investment play pushed them out of the market. Middle Eastern oil producers were persuaded to abandon plans requiring payment in silver or gold. From the brink of monetary disaster, industrial nations were able to take control of their money supplies and rein in prices. The massive move in precious metals between 1979 and 1980 instilled a dream in the hearts and minds of investors. Even today, there are those who long for a return to the "go-go years" for precious metals.

WHAT A METALS-BASED SYSTEM WOULD MEAN TODAY

However, if the world returns to a metals-based system, gold and silver investors could receive an unpleasant shock. First, consider the circumstances that might cause a return to silver and gold. Surely, such a move would follow a confidence crisis. Governments would move to secure supplies. Confiscation is not beyond probability. If citizens were allowed to keep gold and silver, their value might be aligned to new paper, which could actually devalue holdings. In other words, any return to precious metals for monetary backing will not automatically favor investing. On the other hand, a monetary panic is exactly the time to move into precious metals. While currencies are being redesigned, gold and silver may be the only assets maintaining value. During any transition from panic to calm, precious metals offer an insurance policy that has been reasonably tested throughout history.

Absent a monetary crisis, it's doubtful whether there is any immediate incentive for the world to return to metals-backed currency. Yet the potential for a global monetary meltdown should not be taken lightly. Not long ago, a group of intellectuals predicted the world would run out of fuel and food by the year 2100. Based on the most sophisticated computer models and available information, the world was on a collision course with raw material shortages and disaster. Memories are short. At the height of the post-Energy Crisis trauma, world leaders braced for a continued trend of increasing scarcity and associated economic woes. However, the predicted economic pall never came to be. The patient was miraculously cured. So far, the medicine has been increasing efficiency. Yet people are not assured technology will keep pace with global demand.

In addition, the global monetary system survived a series of illnesses which included the Third World Debt Crisis, the U.S. Savings & Loan Crisis, West Germany's absorption of East Germany, the Commonwealth of Independent States Economic Crisis, the Japanese Real Estate and Banking Crisis and the list goes on. Any of these attacks on global financial stability could have triggered panic. Interestingly, the investing and consuming public has refused to join in any mass hysteria despite the magnitude of these various problems. One potent elixir against chaos has been information.

When well informed, people are less inclined to panic. Today's communication is more rapid, more accurate, and more available than ever before. Television spans borders and the Internet allows free communication with few restrictions. As long as we know a solution to a problem is under consideration, we can wait for an outcome. Although communication has given us a new lease on economic stability, it does not eliminate all potential for an ultimate crisis. There remains the possibility governments will lose control over a delicately balanced system of global confidence.

Another important factor in the new world order is the treatment of money as a commodity. Silver and gold are not the only vehicles placed within the "commodity" category. Most of us are aware that currencies can be traded—bought and sold—in the same manner as are gold, silver, wheat, and pork bellies. The value of a currency is a function of the country's risk, productivity, interest rates, and trade balance. It is this very speculation in currency that some believe will sow the seeds of economic ruin. Intercurrency volatility during the past twenty years has grown several hundred percent. In 1995–96, ten percent swings in intercurrency parities were common. More impressively, these swings could take place in less than a quarter year. Figure 2–1 illustrates

F I G U R E 2–1

The U.S. Dollar Index is traded on the Financial Exchange division of the New York Cotton & Juice Exchange. It is an index based on a weighted basket of foreign (non-U.S.) currencies. See how this index varied in just over a one-year period.

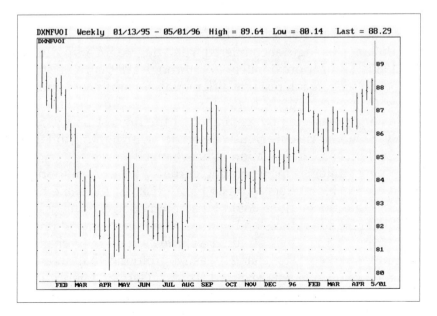

how the U.S. dollar performed on an indexed basis against a basket of foreign currencies.

CHANGES IN CURRENCY MARKETS

Although necessity is the mother of invention, hedge and "risk-aversion" strategies may become hard pressed to deal with excessive volatility. At some point, currency parity can wipe out import and export profit margins. There may come a time when international trade demands a more constant means for exchanging goods and services across borders. Is there hope for silver and gold?

Believe it or not, today people exist in a unique economic environment. There are no rules to follow and no historical perspectives for comfort. During the 1970s, currency traders operated on the principle that any government forced to raise interest rates was in economic trouble. Higher interest rates were used to curb spending and fight inflation. Rising interest rates were a warning to exit one currency in favor of another whose issuing country had more stability. Thus, rising interest rates adversely affected currency parity. If the United Kingdom increased interest rates relative to the United States, it was likely the pound would fall against the dollar. This logic encountered a 180-degree reversal during the 1980s. From approximately 1982 through 1989, currency traders began seeking interest rate differentials for arbitrage opportunities. Countries with the highest interest rates provided the best yields and, consequently, commanded the highest parity. Suddenly, economic risk previously associated with fighting inflation was no longer a consideration. What changed?

New strategies incorporating currency futures and options began to enable traders to offset parity risk. At the same time, interest rate fluctuations could be accommodated using associated interest rate futures and options. The invention and implementation of these new trading vehicles structurally changed currency markets. The change was so profound that an entire trading philosophy was reversed. Thus, if German interest rates became more favorable than United States rates, a trader could buy German bonds denominated in deutsche marks. At the same time, any currency risk could be hedged with a sale of futures or the purchase of deutsche mark put options. Coincidentally, this is not the strategy professional traders use. Obviously, if there is a strong correlation between rising interest rates and rising currency parity, the hedge would be sure to lose. The important point to recognize is that the transaction works because hedge tools are available.

Now billions of U.S. dollars, British pounds, deutsche marks, Japanese yen, Swiss francs, French francs, Australian dollars, Canadian dollars, Mexican pesos, Brazilian reals, and dozens of other currencies exchange hands every day at different parities. Currency trading is a multitrillion dollar business. Parity changes are the lifeblood of traders in some of the largest financial institutions. The entire currency trading arena was born out of structural changes in the 1970s that allowed world currencies to float.

As quickly as the world of bullion-backed currencies evaporated into floating exchange rates, the scene can revert to its metals-backed tradition. For example, the European Common Market that evolved into the European Community (EC) (now the European Union) began designing a cooperative central banking system to create a common currency during the 1980s. An essential step was the Maastricht Treaty, which attempted to hold member currencies within limited parity ranges while setting goals for inflation, government debt, and an agreement to join in a common currency unit.

Thus was born the concept of the ECU—European Currency Unit. Although the currency unit is reflected by a basket of member currencies, the plan merges into a common currency called the Euro. This implies the possible dissolution of individual currency markets. As of 1997, a single European currency was still a concept more than reality, and the debate over a "real ECU" or parity ECU continued. Could an actual Euro bill go into circulation or would individual currencies be valued against the Euro? Understand that a single European currency forecloses some cross-parity speculation. Thus, the multibillion dollar European currency trade could become extinct.

SUPPLY AND DEMAND

If organizations can merge billions of British pounds, Swiss francs, deutsche marks, French francs, Italian lire, and other European currencies into a single unit, why not return to gold and silver monetary standards? Presently, the answer remains, "limited supplies." If the value of all the world's currencies was divided into the global gold inventory, an ounce of gold would have a book value exceeding $200,000 per ounce. If economists created parity only with U.S. dollars, gold would still have a value in excess of $50,000 per ounce. Some economists believe such values are feasible for international transactions. In other words, an ounce of gold would be the same as a $200,000 bill. But, as a common money, this metal won't fit the bill—or, the bill won't fit the money. Silver is a significantly better candidate. Unfortunately, today's industrial demand for silver consumes too much to allow any accumulation of "free stocks." These are supplies that are not needed for particular applications. As later chapters show, technology may rapidly change the situation for silver and gold.

Symbolic parity is not beyond reality. It may be possible to link silver and gold to a single Global Currency Unit (GCU). There is nothing that says accounting cannot be done on a fractional basis to accommodate a GCU. Investors might trade in 1/200,000th of an ounce.

This scenario would raise other issues. First, some believe economies could see tremendous economic dislocation whereby gold- and silver-producing nations would have a significant advantage over nonproducers. This theory has already been tested false. Under such an assumption, South Africa should be one of the world's wealthiest nations. It wasn't during the Golden Era and it is not today. Japan, with virtually no gold production and the lowest central bank reserves, flourished. In fact, Japan became an economic superpower with very few natural resources, period! Certainly, there may be a windfall on the initial sale of gold and silver production. Thereafter, economic strength moves supplies between nations. Most importantly, who would own the mines? Knowledgeable investors would want stock in every gold and silver mine they could get their hands on for the first ten transitional years. Could you imagine the profit margins? Realistically, production would come under some governmental control.

It should not be difficult to understand why the world was forced off a two-tiered, metals-based monetary system. Economic progress was to blame. There may always be individuals who believe economies should return to gold and silver money. However, to understand the new precious metals markets, investors must accept the reality that precious metals don't make good money—for now.

Although gold and silver may not be appropriate monetary instruments in today's economic systems, they still represent a "value of last resort." In countries with unstable economies, the person who owns gold will be protected against currency devaluations and economic disaster. Gold is a portable, tangible asset. Further, there is an implied "gold standard" because anyone can easily convert this metal into any currency. In some respects, the cliché stands, "Nothing is as good as gold!"

Finally, consider that central banks continue holding millions of ounces of gold as "reserves." Figure 2–2 plots the approximate reserves of the major industrial nations. If, indeed, the world has abandoned gold as a monetary standard, why is it still hoarded as a reserve asset? The answer is obvious. If all else fails, gold will retain its monetary value. The fact that huge gold reserves exist plays heavily on the day-to-day market. Rumors of possible divestiture supported by some central bank sales like Belgium, Australia, and Portugal have had a depressing effect upon prices. Certainly, any joint move to sell gold reserves will flood the market. However, in the aftermath of such an event, citizens would be wise to accumulate their own "personal reserves."

As later chapters show, gold and silver production is accelerating. The speed with which technology and discovery increase production could determine whether it will be feasible to return to some "remonetization" of precious metals. Because reserve balances already fluctuate with changing currency parities, economists have a basis for accepting that gold and silver can be used as reserve assets. Much will depend on a new generation of world leaders who are assuming power as you read this book. Certainly, Baby Boomers are familiar with events like the Great Depression

F I G U R E   2-2

Central Bank Estimated Gold Reserves-1994

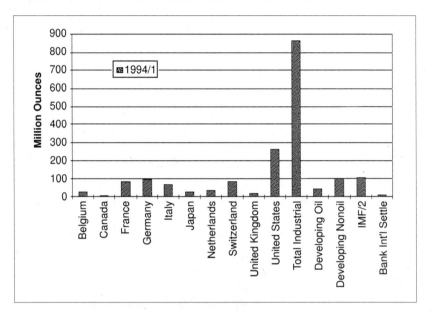

from stories their parents or grandparents told. Those born between 1940 and 1975 lived through the legalization of possessing bulk gold in 1975 but may not have fully appreciated the significance of that event. Anyone born after 1965 can hardly remember the Energy Crisis of the early 1970s. As "the new generation" takes power, there may be reluctance to return to past standards. In particular, individuals in the investment industry have seen paper assets soar while precious metals have had lackluster performance. If new leaders believe more can be made trading paper than holding gold reserves, there could be a move to dump "nonperforming assets" in favor of government participation in financial markets. After all, many a projection of the U.S. Social Security system has been made assuming simple "dollar averaging" investing in the Dow Industrial Average or Standard & Poor's 500 stocks. Indeed, the system would be more than fully funded had the U.S. government been able to make such commitments.

F I G U R E   2-3

Gold prices. Compare 1991–1992 to the ten years
from 1986 to 1996 to show central bank sales did
not violate the overall price range.

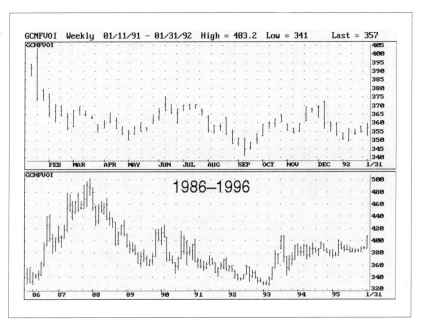

What if central banks did divest gold and silver holdings?
Would we really see a massive decline in prices? In 1991 and 1992
Belgium liquidated approximately 200 tons of gold while the
Netherlands sold 400 tons. Within the same period, sales by
Russia and the Middle East added another 300 tons to the market.
The purpose was to bring gold reserves in line with other EC
member nations—and to raise cash. Figure 2–3 charts the gold
price through these two years in comparison with a spanning
ten-year period. Notice that there was no significant sell-off. The
free market was comfortably able to absorb the additional supplies. It is true that 600 tons is far less than an estimated 40,000
held by central banks. However, it is inconceivable that we would
see such imprudence as a simultaneous global dumping.

What does the future hold for gold and silver as monetary instruments? World leaders have conspicuously avoided any specific reference to gold as a reserve asset. Gold is neither an official reserve nor a nonreserve. It is simply there, held in central bank vaults. As previously mentioned, central banks held an estimated 35,000 to 40,000 tons of gold as of 1994. Each ton represents 32,150 troy ounces. Assuming the higher 40,000-ton estimate with a price of $400 per ounce, 1994 bank reserves had a value of $514.4 billion. The U.S. Gross Domestic Product alone was several trillions. The enormous economic expansion from 1900 through the present time has required an equally large increase in our global monetary base. Obviously, gold supplies have not kept pace with this growth. According to Gold Fields Mineral Services, Ltd., net "official purchases" reversed in 1989 to become "net official sales." Figure 2–4 shows the trend from 1986 through 1995.

Clearly a transition took place in the mid-1980s that moved industrialized nations from net accumulators to net distributors. Conceivably, official sales depressed prices from the mid-1980s forward. This has been a major argument presented by gold

F I G U R E   2–4

Net accumulation and distribution of gold by "official" entities 1986–95.

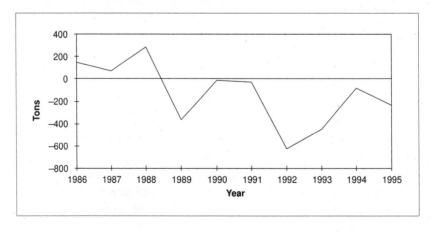

Bar hoarding kept pace with official dishoarding
from 1986 to 1995.

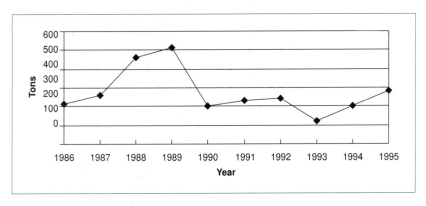

advocates. They claim the "real" gold price is obscured by official
sales that artificially distort supply. As long as official inventories
hang over the market, gold's performance will be distorted.

By smoothing the sales from 1986 through 1995, a discernible
trend can be noted toward increasing official gold divestiture. The
further central banks move away from gold, the more difficult it
will be to return to any gold standard. What is interesting about
the equation is the degree to which private gold hoarding has kept
pace with official liquidations. Over the same time period from
1986 through 1995, gold bars were steadily accumulated. Bar
hoarding is an important barometer of investment demand. Figure 2–5 illustrates gold bar accumulation.

Total net official sales distributed 1,284 tons of gold from
1986 through 1995, whereas bar hoarding absorbed 2,733. Therefore, net investment accumulation was more than twice as much
as official distribution. In the meantime, official world mine production has been steadily adding to supplies, as apparent in
Figure 2–6.

Approximately 25 percent of current gold production is
being hoarded. At this rate, total accumulation will remain too
slow to appreciably increase the hoard to levels required for

Gold production increased at a modest rate from
1986 to 1995.

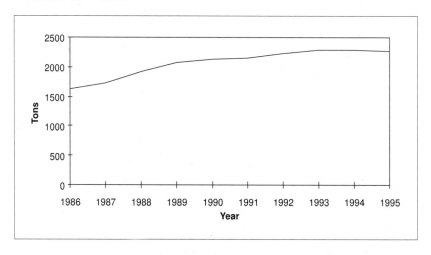

monetary use within any reasonable time. Consider that even if
official holdings doubled to 80,000 tons, they would tally to
slightly more than $1 trillion in value at $400 an ounce. The trend
in gold discoveries and mining technology should lead to increasing output that can double every five to ten years. At that rate, it
would take ten to twenty years to produce the amount held in
official hands as of 1995.

The only circumstance that could provide an environment
conducive for a return to a gold standard seems to be a deflationary spiral. Nations would need a massive contraction in the global
monetary base that could allow a realignment to gold at reasonable levels. Believe it or not, such a deflation was predicted by
popular analysts to occur by the mid-1990s. Robert Prechter, the
man credited with reviving the Elliott Wave Theory, published a
small text foretelling the end of the economic boom and the
coming of a huge economic implosion. If you believe in the Grand
Cycle, gold could return as money by the year 2020. At that point,
the global economic cycle should have bottomed out.

If governments take the implosion theory seriously, we
could see a change in net accumulation patterns moving into the

first decade of the millennium. What should you do if you are interested in riding the next gold wave? My instincts tell me official accumulation and distribution patterns will be critical. At the first sign of a monetary meltdown, you can be sure central banks will move to protect themselves with something more than intergovernmental promises. Gold will be the cornerstone for stability. But don't be surprised if the official price is far less than the market price if any monetary decision is made to bring back the yellow metal.

Given restricted gold supplies, isn't it more likely the world will adopt a bimetallic monetary standard if government reserves return to metal? What about silver? Official silver inventories could be accumulated quickly to supplement gold reserves. First, the price is right. Second, if there were an acceleration in the amount of silver freed by a move away from photographic film, there would be more of an incentive to use a gold/silver parity rather than a single metal. Figure 2–7 charts world silver production in tons from 1979 through 1994.

F I G U R E 2–7

Global silver output increased through 1990 before encountering a slowdown. Projections suggest a resumption of the upward momentum.

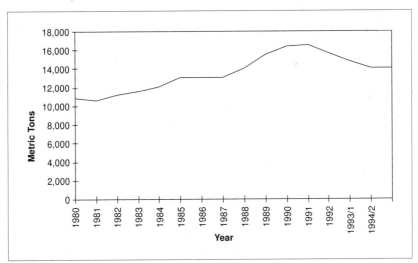

Projections based on economic stability in Chile and Peru as well as other Third World producing nations actually show a resumption in the production uptrend from 1997 forward. This trend is always debatable and circumstances can always change, but we can assume 20,000 metric tons of production moving forward from the year 2000. Approximately 33 percent of annual silver production has been used for photography. There could be a progressive increase in "free stocks" if there were a technological displacement of silver. At $5 per ounce, a metric ton of silver is valued at $160,750. At 20,000 metric tons of production, the value of one year's output at $5 is $3.215 billion.

Again, this amount is fractional compared with the world monetary base. Even if the world's annual silver production rose by a third, nations would hardly have sufficient metal to accommodate current economies without regard for economic growth. Further, official silver reserves are not sufficient as monetary assets. Government accumulations would need to be large, indeed, before nations could comfortably go into a bimetallic system. When the United States dissolved silver convertibility, there were approximately 1.7 billion ounces held by the U.S. Treasury. This amounts to only $8.5 billion at $5 per ounce.

The debate over metal as money will rage and simmer for years to come. The only positive conclusion is that huge adjustments in global economic systems and thinking would be required to inspire economic leaders to adopt a metallic standard. Either an exceedingly fine fractional system using substantial values would need to be in place ($200,000 per ounce of gold and some ratio for silver), or the world would have to undergo a massive monetary contraction. As of this writing, the prospects for metal as money remain dim.

CHAPTER 3

Are Precious Metals Investments?

There are many different views on the definition of an investment. In general, an *investment* is a sacrifice of present utility or effort in return for future gain. You can invest your time in a project because you anticipate some form of reward. A person invests money in financial vehicles to achieve an increased future value. Some invest in art for both the pleasure of its beauty and potential monetary appreciation. However, more financially specific investing deals with a process that encompasses a monetary commitment related to an *expected value*. Expected value is commonly called the *return*. The degree to which the investor's expectations are realized is associated with risk. The amount placed at risk is called *exposure.*

These are important terms and concepts because they are often misunderstood and misused. For example, options have become popular. An *option* is the right, but not the obligation, to buy or sell something at a predetermined price, called the *strike*. An option applies during a specified time period, called the *duration.* The cost of this privilege is called the *premium.*

WHAT THE JARGON MEANS

A common sales practice is to represent options as "limited risk." A salesperson may explain that a silver option being offered has a $6 strike, costs only $500 in premium, and expires in December. He or she may tell you that your risk is limited because the most you can lose is the $500 in premium. Is this true?

If the chance silver can achieve a price exceeding $6 an ounce between the time you buy your option and its expiration is zero, your "risk" is actually 100 percent. In addition, silver must move above $6 by more than your $500 premium before you can make money as of the expiration. Thus, the only limit in the transaction is on your exposure. It is true that the most you can lose is $500. However, the entire concept of "limited risk" is highly misleading. In precious metals markets, this is a particular concern. Countless scams have been designed around high premium options that have little or no chance of ever appreciating in value. As this chapter shows, there are correct strategies and wrong strategies for using options on precious metals.

INVESTMENTS AS HAVING BOTH INCOME POTENTIAL AND UNDERLYING VALUE

With these thoughts in mind, are precious metals investments? Certainly, there have been periods when buying silver, gold, platinum, and palladium could provide speculative gain. Yet in the long run, metals have not performed as good investments. First, metals have no intrinsic yield. Stocks, bonds, and real estate all have associated cash flows or "income" potential. Stocks yield dividends. Bonds return interest. Real estate generates rent. In addition to cash flow, the underlying value of income-generating investments can increase. In fact, increasing value is correlated with cash flow potential. This is why a stock's price-to-earnings (P/E) ratio is considered so important. Because physical precious metals have no yield, their value is solely based on supply and demand.

In approaching the new precious metals markets, it is important to avoid old clichés. There is a popular correlation between an ounce of gold and the price of a good suit, which demonstrates that gold has maintained a stable purchasing power despite inflation. This parallel confuses a good "store of value" with a good appreciating investment. Yes, gold may have kept pace with inflation. But the purpose of investing is to move appreciably *ahead* of inflation to accumulate wealth. There is also the story of the man who had 2,000 ounces of gold and sold just two ounces per month. Plotting the sale against gold prices, he has been able to live a comfortable life for the past 1,000 months (83 years). Compare this gentleman with Warren Buffet, who went from having virtually nothing to more than $14 billion in 1996 and I believe the point is made. The first guy would have been better off selling his gold and investing in the market!

Precious Metals as Commodities
Rather than Investments

Since 1987 there has been a growing consensus that precious metals are not investments, but commodities. As with any other commodity, the value of silver, gold, and the platinum group will be determined by the amount mined and global demand. This thinking implies that metals can provide only "speculative" opportunity rather than investment potential.

The difference between speculation and investing is subtle. Speculation is associated with quick gain. Speculative financial vehicles are "traded" rather than held. Certainly, you can make money buying low and selling high. Yet, if you compare the purchase of the Dow Index stocks against a comparable amount of gold or silver over any ten-year period, you will find that equities outperform metals as investments (see Figure 3–1). Equities experience an overall appreciation known as the *secular trend*. Although corrections can be related to recessions or inflation, stocks and bonds continue as more stable investments.

Before silver and gold were decoupled from their monetary roles, these metals established international currency parities. The U.S. dollar derived its intrinsic value from its gold parity of $35 per ounce. If parity cannot change, then gold will inflate along

F I G U R E   3–1

Gold versus the Dow. When gold and the Dow are
compared during a ten-year span, it is clear that
gold values remained static while stocks in the Dow
Index substantially appreciated.

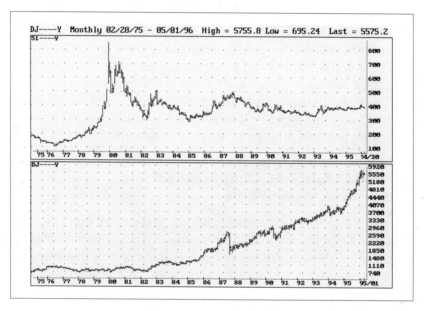

with the dollar or any other currency if the commodity price index
or consumer price index is rising. Compare the progress of gold
against the Dow Industrial Average since ownership of gold by
U.S. citizens was reestablished 1975 (Figure 3–1). A historical
overview reveals that the Energy Crisis during the early 1970s
precipitated the Nixon era "stagflation." Americans experienced
a recession and inflation reflected by poor stock market performance and soaring precious metals prices. Thereafter, the world
began adjusting for a purely paper system that pushed equity and
bond values higher while removing incentives for owning precious metals. The essential difference between paper assets and
physical metals is the earning potential. Companies earn money,
which translates into dividends. Bonds provide a steady stream

of interest revenue. Precious metals can make money for the average investor only if the metals' value appreciates and holdings are liquidated.

The nineteenth-century gold and silver boom generated income for producers, as well as those selling picks, shovels, jackasses, covered wagons, and train tickets. As previously mentioned, the Gold Rush continues today. Not surprisingly, the money makers are still producers. Likewise, the best precious metals investments have been exploration and mining stocks. The fantastic performance of mining stocks during the 1980s and 1990s can be directly correlated with technological advancements and strong product demand. The costs of extraction and processing steadily declined while the prices remained reasonably stable. Profit margins grew along with volume. Huge price advances of 1979-80 presented enormous speculative opportunities. Gold prices rocketed from $150 an ounce to more than $800. Figure 3–2 plots gold prices (above) in U.S. dollars from 1975 through 1982. Clearly, the profit potential was enormous if one had the foresight to divest just after the peak. Without such insight, gold failed miserably as an "investment." Silver's performance was parallel as illustrated by the price chart for the same period in the lower half of Figure 3–2.

Reasons for the Surge of the 1970s

What made precious metals such speculative successes toward the end of the 1970s? One reason was the legalization of gold in the United States. There was a new demand for gold and a bandwagon effect in silver, platinum, and palladium. Further, the Cold War encouraged rumors of strategic metals shortages that focused on platinum, palladium, and rhodium (Figure 3–3). The Soviet Union was the largest producer behind South Africa. Finally, the world was making a difficult and uncertain transition away from metals-backed currency during a highly inflationary and politically tenuous period. Within a single decade, the world experienced the highest prices for grain, energy, coffee, sugar, pork, beef, metals, and other commodities. On an inflation-adjusted basis, these price records still stood as of 1996.

F I G U R E 3-2

Inflation and monetary uncertainty spiked silver
(above) and gold (below) to record-high prices
during 1979–80.

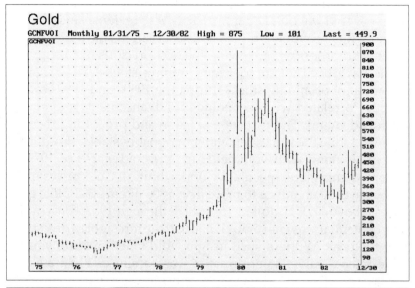

Gold

GCNFVOI   Monthly 01/31/75 - 12/30/82 High = 875   Low = 101   Last = 449.9

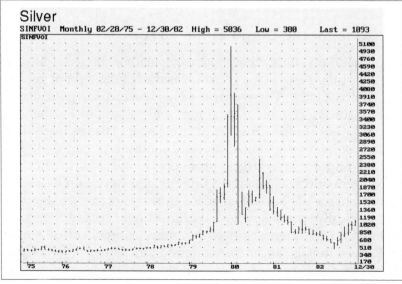

Silver

SINFVOI   Monthly 02/28/75 - 12/30/82 High = 5036   Low = 380   Last = 1093

F I G U R E 3–3

Platinum followed gold and silver to record highs in
the same 1979–80 time span.

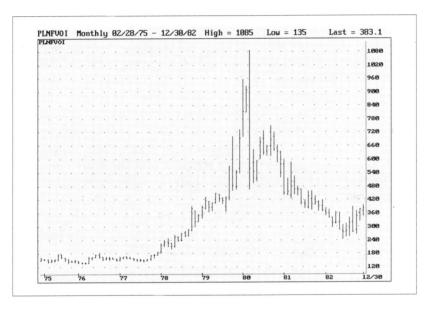

PLNFVOI Monthly 02/28/75 – 12/30/82 High = 1005 Low = 135 Last = 383.1

It is important to realize that the unprecedented surge in
precious metals from 1979 through the beginning of 1980 was the
beginning of the second major structural change to the precious
metals market following the divorce with monetary standards.
Obviously, the first structural change was the move from fixed to
floating prices for gold and silver parity. Thereafter, economic
incentives to explore for and mine gold and silver remained weak
until prices moved sharply higher. Mining costs for gold were
between $80 and $150 per ounce in 1975. From the time gold
opened at just under $200 in 1975 through the first half of 1976,
prices sharply declined to support at just $100 an ounce. This was
attributed to poor investor interest and the slow economy. In
addition, U.S. Treasury sales depressed prices from 1975 through
1976. Silver traded in a narrow range between $3.75 and $5. At the
same time, costs had risen from 1969 through 1975 because of the

Energy Crisis and global inflation. It was not particularly profitable to operate mines.

As demand heated up, new supplies were flat. By 1978, the picture was looking much brighter. At more than $250 an ounce for gold and $5.50 for silver, there was a better incentive to expand marginal production up to a cost point of approximately $200 for gold and $3.75 for silver. It doesn't take a genius to understand that when prices rocket to more than $850 for gold and close to $50 for silver, producers will seek every possible way to squeeze out more production. New technology used solvents to remove trace amounts of metal from low-grade ores unworthy of consideration prior to the price explosion. In time, these extraction techniques became increasingly efficient and the entire production environment changed. Deep-shaft mining gave way to surface strip mines. By-product production of silver and gold became the major component in growing production. Although precious metals prices were rising, so were prices of the base metals like copper, tin, zinc, lead, aluminum, and nickel. Each of these metals increased precious metal by-product production.

On the flip side of the equation, industrial users were forced to rapidly seek alternatives to silver, gold, platinum, and palladium. The huge price surge toward the end of the 1970s became the catalyst for finding substitutes for gold coatings on glass, gold dental materials, electrical contacts, jewelry, and other applications. Use of silver brazing materials, mirroring, electronics, tableware, and jewelry also came under attack. A huge recycling/scrap business was born and there were actual wars over who would collect X-ray negatives from hospitals and old film from lithographic printers.

The combination of better production, better exploration, new discoveries, better recovery, and alternative materials structurally changed the way the world produced and used precious metals. Suddenly, there were increasing supplies at increasing rates. From 1980 to 1990, the United States increased its gold output by 1,000 percent. There was ten times more gold being produced in less than a decade. South Carolina went from being a nonproducing state to the ninth-largest gold producer within twelve years based on new mining and extraction technologies.

Of course, this pace was duplicated in other parts of the world. For those who follow precious metals, this is a significant point. Throughout the 1980s there were countless schemes that lifted tens of millions of dollars out of unsuspecting pockets using the pitch that the world faced a pending shortage of silver and gold. There was the threat of a Soviet strategic metals embargo. There was the China Silver Syndrome, in which the People's Republic was going to corner the entire world production. The list of fables is almost endless. Throughout this period, very few news stories carried the truth about surging supplies.

Hitting the Skids in the 1980s

Unfortunately, investors wanted to hear that gold and silver would resume their upward spiral. Those who missed the moves of the 1970s were anxious for a repeat performance. In other words, people were easy victims. Also, inflation continued into the 1980s. It took half that decade and unprecedented interest rates to bring prices under control. This represented a final structural change that substantially reduced the roles of gold and silver as inflation hedges. Although introduced in 1972, currency futures did not gain in popularity until the development of other financial futures and options contracts. The Chicago Board of Trade announced the first interest rate futures contract with the Ginnie Mae. Thereafter came T-bills, T-notes, T-bonds, Eurodollars, and muni bonds. Suddenly, there was a paper alternative to gold and silver. If inflation were present, the sale of interest rate futures would ride the wave of rising interest rates to offset exposure. The deterioration of any currency could be countered by selling the appropriate futures contracts short or buying put options. These "derivative" vehicles obviated the need to use gold and silver.

Equally important, paper markets were more liquid and easier to use. Understand that the physical precious metals markets are slow and cumbersome. It takes time to transfer and move metals. They must be insured and assayed. If batches are transported, time and expense are involved. Simply put, trading large amounts of physical gold, silver, platinum, or palladium is not an investment activity for the "modern age of paper markets."

Once the role of gold and silver as an inflation hedge diminished, interest in precious metals became diluted. Certainly, high interest yields in the 1980s made government debt more attractive than holding silver or gold bars. The stock market's bull trend also offered far better returns than precious metals. Thus, even attitudes toward gold and silver structurally changed. Particular "crisis events" that would have pushed investors toward gold and silver failed to influence prices. Many believe the Falklands War between the United Kingdom and Argentina was pivotal. At the onset, gold surged more than $25 an ounce. However, enthusiasm for gold and silver immediately reversed. When the Soviet Union shot down a Korean airliner, metals did not respond. The August 1990 invasion of Kuwait by Iraq had a modest influence upon gold and silver. The subsequent Gulf War was a precious metals yawn compared with the reaction one would have expected in the late 1970s. Investors became less interested in moving into metals because the "crisis hedge" was no longer valid. In fact, stocks and bonds had more pronounced and long-lasting reactions to crisis as illustrated by the impressive U.S. equity market recovery on the initiation of Operation Desert Storm in January of 1991 (Figure 3–4).

Well, if precious metals are not good investments, shouldn't the book end here? After all, history shows gold and silver have not performed well over time. Recent events clearly indicate investors have abandoned precious metals as a crisis hedge. New derivative markets permit strategies to offset inflation and deflation. Central banks have eliminated charters and language linking gold to the monetary base as a "reserve asset." *The New York Times* and *The Wall Street Journal* no longer carry gold as one of their economic indicators. Technology is finding ways to substitute lower-cost materials for gold, silver, platinum, and palladium. What purpose can precious metals serve other than their intrinsic psychological appeal?

MINING AS THE KEY TO VALUE IN THE 1990s

Anyone familiar with precious metals should know gold mining stocks were among the best performers during the latter half of the 1980s and through the 1990s. Gold stock funds outpaced the

FIGURE 3-4

The S&P surged in response to Desert Storm to demonstrate how equities were more responsive than precious metals during this crisis.

S&P 500 and Dow Industrial Average by hefty margins. Rather than abandon gold, the world has embraced this metal and, in reality, demand is keeping pace with production. The hottest new issues are not just technology stocks related to the Internet and medical advances. Each time there is a new gold discovery, investors flock to the issue with fists full of dollars. Why the investment interest? The fact is that today's gold mining is highly profitable. There are few heavy industries in which spreads between production costs and selling prices are so wide and getting wider. There are few products that have such continuous demand and stable "relative" prices. Basically, gold is good business.

Silver is also good business. Today, most silver is produced as a by-product of other metals. Silver represents additional "marginal profit" on other metal production. If silver prices rise, marginal profits follow. Platinum is a unique metal. Far more rare than gold and silver, platinum is the cornerstone of value in terms of industrial demand. Although there are technological threats to major platinum applications like automotive catalytic converters, new technologies like fuel cells and heavy water fusion are likely to fill demand gaps. Finally, palladium has excellent prospects as a platinum substitute in catalytic devices and as the metal involved in the highly questioned "cold fusion" technology. Taken as a group, precious metals are extremely good commodities.

There are many ways to invest and speculate in commodities. Depending on characteristics, you can invest in the means for production. When you buy a share of RJR Nabisco, you are participating in the production and distribution of food and tobacco products. When you invest in North American Palladium on the NASD small cap market, you are participating in the production and distribution of palladium. When you buy stock in Placer Dome, you are investing in gold production and distribution. Therefore, it is important to understand the commodities you are backing through your equity investments. That is why you must understand the new precious metals markets. How can you properly evaluate a food company relative to a precious metals producer? Should you buy utilities or gold stocks?

Precious metals have the unique characteristic of being "semiconsumables." Unlike crude oil or agricultural products, a portion of each year's precious metals production is hoarded. In the case of gold, the majority is hoarded as bars, coins, and jewelry. This accumulation plays a critical role in the long-term prospects for precious metals. The process is a throwback to the monetary link and is likely to maintain a stability not found in other commodities. All signs point to a strong future for gold, silver, platinum, and palladium. This suggests that you will have investment opportunities in stocks of producer companies and speculative opportunities in futures and options markets. In addition, the same derivative vehicles and strategies that dulled the luster of physical metals markets can brighten their comeback. It is possible to use gold and silver as the foundation for yield-bearing programs. Just as banks may trade options against cash balances, so can an investor trade against gold and silver inventories. In fact, we could see precious metals producers using production as "backing" for market strategies rather than just selling into the physical market.

As semiconsumables, precious metals will always maintain roles as "a store of value." They are still assets of last resort. In the coming years, humanity will see enormous technological and political change, and probably the most rapid age of human development in history. Some say humans are on a road to disaster. Frankly, if the world develops living standards set by the United States and Western Europe, Mother Earth will be nothing more than a revolving cinder by the end of the twenty-first century. If the pace of global industrial development continues, doomsayers will finally be vindicated. Obviously, something must change.

Technology must address population and progress. As later chapters reveal, platinum and palladium may play significant roles in changing the way people power the world. Although still highly controversial, new technologies based on special characteristics of platinum group elements may provide solutions to an inevitable energy-related crisis. How does this impact precious metals? The most obvious effect will be rising values for the platinum group. If, indeed, cold fusion based on palladium becomes a reality, this metal could become the most valuable on earth. Given platinum's complementary role in the process announced by Pons and Fleischmann in March of 1989, investors could see equal opportunities for speculative gain. Stocks of platinum-producing companies would have extraordinary performance. Companies developing the new technology will offer equally impressive investment opportunity. All the while, precious metals, as a group, will be viewed as ultimate "hard assets" that maintain value.

Before the book moves on to new precious metals strategies, it is important to address the assertion by many asset managers and financial planners that some gold belongs in every portfolio. The theory is that gold stabilizes a portfolio and acts as an insurance policy against monetary catastrophe. I have seen recommendations for gold holdings ranging from 5 percent to 10 percent of total financial assets. This means that an individual with net financial assets of $100,000 should have between $5,000 and $10,000 in gold. This philosophy assumes that gold will perform during high inflation or a paper confidence crisis. However, assumptions are based on gold's performance during the 1970s and early 1980s. This approach doesn't consider new hedge strategies using derivatives in interest rates and currencies. There are several reasons why holding physical gold should be questioned. Aside from risks associated with safekeeping, why should you hold a nonperforming asset?

For those living in Western Europe, the United States, and developed nations of the Pacific Rim, the need for a monetary hedge is questionable. Any 10 percent investment in gold bars or coins significantly underperformed the stock market, bonds, and gold stocks through the 1980s and 1990s. The most conservative view can develop a logical argument favoring the performance sacrifice in return for security. However, investors are not the same as central banks. Investors have no need for reserve assets. If the time to own gold is during a monetary crisis, the market is sufficiently liquid to enter when instability appears to approach. Modern inflations are not likely to appear overnight. If a progressive rise in the Consumer Price Index develops, a move into precious metals may be justified while inflation is present. However, be aware that gold may not be as sensitive to inflation today as it was in the 1970s and 1980s.

PRECIOUS METALS AS PERFORMING ASSETS

Strategically, it is possible to turn metals into performing assets. This is where the line between speculation and investing becomes blurred. The key is to recognize the dynamics of precious metals markets have changed. We are dealing in new environments with new rules. Today, the traditionalist can "have his cake and eat it, too." If you hold physical gold, you can earn money on your inventory. If you know prices will remain stable, you can develop strategies that take advantage of flat price action. If silver persists in trading within a wide but limited price range, you have a way to make exciting gains with limited risk and exposure.

With the creation of new markets, financial vehicles, and strategies, precious metals could actually become better "investments" than they have ever been in the past. I find this somewhat humorous because gold and silver advocates spend millions each year to promote investing in gold and silver. The World Gold Council represents producers around the globe and publishes detailed academic studies and reports dealing with the monetary aspects of this single metal. The Gold Institute and Silver Institute, located in Washington, D.C., actively promotes gold and silver investing. The Platinum Guild and Johnson Matthey call attention to the benefits of owning platinum. These organizations do an excellent job of collecting, digesting, and distributing information. Most literature directed toward investors focuses on owning gold with sidebars on using futures, options, mining stocks, and leveraged transactions. There is little information about using gold and silver inventories to implement specific investment strategies.

Change is often difficult. We are all influenced by past perspectives. Thus, it is difficult to divorce from traditional gold and silver thinking. You can view precious metals as money, investments, an insurance policy, a store of value, or as collectibles. The new metals markets combine past traditions with modern strategies. Of course, the global economic environment can change, and probably will. When you consider using new approaches, always keep in mind how and why conditions can change. A good fundamental background should help. So will an open mind!

CHAPTER 4

New Strategies for New Markets

Even central banks know gold inventories should have income-generating potential. During the past several years, a system of loaning gold at nominal interest rates has been developed to help producers and consumers hedge. The gold "loan rate" is the interest charged on these transactions that permits the borrowing of inventory for replacement at some future date. Because gold is held as a reserve asset, the "opportunity risk" on the part of the lender is theoretical. There is no intention to part with the inventory or speculate on price movements; the gold is simply loaned out with an interest charge.

I refer to structural changes in precious metals markets throughout this text. These changes are important strategy considerations. When Americans carried gold coins in their pockets, the market structure foreclosed investing or speculating. Gold was money, not an investment. The same held true for silver. The postmonetary era brought about speculative potential. U.S. gold futures began trading in 1975. However, U.S. gold options were introduced in 1982. This was after the precious metals frenzy of 1979–80. The introduction of options created entirely new strategies for precious metals investors. Considerable literature on precious metals investing was developed between 1975 and 1981. This material does not necessarily cover the use of option strategies.

CALL OPTIONS

If you own physical gold in excess of 100 ounces, you can accomplish the same type of transaction as institutions that loan gold by selling call options against your inventory. For example, as of August, 1996, an October 400 gold call was quoted at $490 while gold was trading at approximately 39200. Gold options traded on the Commodity Exchange Incorporated (COMEX) division of the New York Mercantile Exchange (NYMEX) represent 100 ounces. Recall the strike price of 400 is the price at which the option buyer can purchase gold. Consider that the value of 100 ounces trading at $392 (39200) per ounce is $39,200. Therefore, the $490 premium represents a 1.25 percent return. This is derived by dividing $490 by the total contract value of $39,200.

If you sold the 400 call, you would collect $490. Of course, timing might yield a better or less attractive premium. October gold options expire in mid-September. Therefore, your 1.25 percent premium is earned between August and September—approximately six weeks. Annualized, these earnings amount to 10.83 percent (divide 1.25 percent by six weeks and multiply by 52).

Option premiums are a function of time, volatility, and proximity. The closer the strike, the more likely it is to be "in the money." This increases premium values. The longer the time period, the higher the premium, under the assumption that time carries risk and associated value. The greater the volatility, the more likely a strike price can be achieved. Over the course of a year, gold can exhibit reasonable volatility and provide healthy option premiums. Options are available for December, February, April, June, August, and October futures expirations. (Options relate to futures contracts.) There are six separate opportunities to sell gold options during the year. Even if the best premiums averaged only 0.5 percent for each expiration, a 3 percent annualized yield would result.

What are the risks and exposures? The inherent risk in owning gold is that its value will decline. You may have purchased your metal at $400 an ounce in March or April of 1996. By September, you lost approximately $15 per ounce or 3.75 percent. Over the same time, you might have sold April, June, August, and October call options for various premiums ranging from $1 to $5. Even with the 3.75 percent decline, there were enough option opportunities to provide a net positive return. Of course, gold prices could plunge. Although it's not historically evident in data during the past 10 years, there is always a possibility the metal could seriously decline in value. Under such circumstances, the question would be whether call options could still provide enough premium to offset falling values. On the other hand, gold prices could rise above your strike price. You would be exposed to losing your gold. In this case, you would still achieve the positive appreciation from the price at the time you sold the option to the strike. Thus, if you sold a $400 call when gold was selling for $385, you would make $15 an ounce plus your premium.

There are defensive strategies that can keep you in the game. As long as people are willing to buy gold options, you can trade against your inventory. This is a form of "covered write." It is called this because your option exposure is offset by your actual gold inventory. Some successful practitioners of this methodology have been accumulating gold during the past decade. Despite the lack of price appreciation, properly timed option selling has yielded comfortable returns ranging between 6 percent and 15 percent per year. At the same time, there is the underlying comfort of knowing you hold the quintessential asset of last resort. In the event gold moves above your call strike, you can buy more gold to replace the amount that will be "called away." Don't forget that you will receive the price associated with your call. In some cases, traders will buy futures to cover the call with a stop at or near the call strike for protection against price failure. It is a balancing act between option premiums and inventory exposure. However, professional traders make money this way.

You do not need a physical gold inventory to practice selling calls. If you have the cash equivalent of a gold inventory, you can sell calls and cover with futures if the strike is exceeded. Under this scenario, you are making your return on cash with the presumption that cash will be used to buy gold or gold futures. Here, your transaction can be leveraged. A gold futures contract might have a margin as low as $1,500 per 100 ounces. A $15 premium on a *covered write* based on futures represents $1,500 on $1,500, or 100 percent. The amount of leverage you use is a subjective decision that should be based on objective criteria. The fact that you may have $1,500 for the futures contract and there is a $15 premium offered does not mean you can afford the exposure. What if you sell a $400 call at $15 and the price moves to $415? Your premium will be wiped out. Any move beyond $415 will cost you $100 for every $1. This is because the futures contract and related option represent 100 ounces of gold.

SELLING A CALL AND BUYING A PUT

On occasion gold moves higher and you will have an opportunity to sell a call while buying a put for a credit. This strategy reduces the amount you make on the call by the amount you must spend on the put. However, you are protected if prices collapse because the call becomes worthless as the put appreciates. Finally, gold may remain confined to a trading range. If the range is wide, and swings from peak to trough are frequent and swift, you might be able to sell both calls and puts above and below the range.

Consider the market from 1993 through 1996 (Figure 4–1). Gold traded in a range between $370 and $400 per ounce. This provided put and call strikes at 360, 370, 380, 390, 400, and 410. Gold options are traded in $10 increments. Few commodities were supported as well as gold during this period. The stability coupled with the possibility of a breakout or bust was just the fuel needed to heat up premiums on a regular basis. Strategically placed sales of calls and puts could have yielded returns in excess of stocks, bonds, real estate, and other investments.

F I G U R E 4–1

Gold price 1993–96. Gold exhibited wide swings above and below the midline of a trading range.

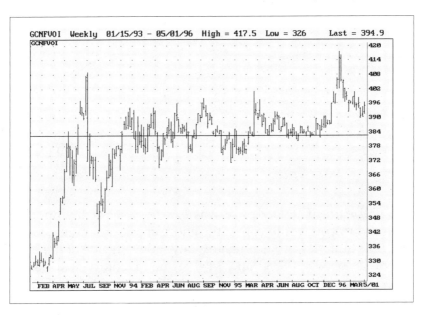

GCNFVOI Weekly 01/15/93 – 05/01/96 High = 417.5 Low = 326 Last = 394.9

BUTTERFLIES AND CONDORS

In addition to covered call writing, there are strategies that can protect inventories against dramatic breakouts or failures. Such strategies apply to holders of physical metal or those anticipating owning metal using a cash reserve. If you own 100 ounces while gold is trading at approximately $390 per ounce, you can sell (write) 390 calls and 390 puts while buying 400 calls and 380 puts. This transaction is commonly referred to as a "butterfly" where the two 390 options are the "body" or "inside options" and the "outside options" are the "wings" (see Figure 4–2). When advantageously placed, premiums earned on the body should exceed the amount paid for the wings. This is called a "credit" transaction. Because only one inside option can be in the money, your exposure is limited to $10 on either side less the credit premium. The closer the price is to the body on expiration, the more premium

F I G U R E   4–2

A Butterfly

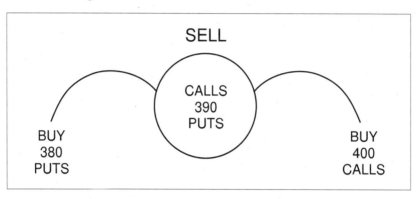

you will earn. If gold's price was exactly $390 at the options' expirations, you would collect the entire credit premium.

The butterfly protects against any move outside of the trading range between $380 and $400. Your inventory will not be called away because you are protected by the $400 call. If gold prices soar, you still own it. For the holder of metal, an alternative strategy is to finance buying a put with the sale of a call at a credit. This protects your gold from a price decline while yielding a premium if the price remains stable. If you bought a 380 put and gold declined below 380, your inventory would be protected by a short futures position. If gold recovered above 380, you would be back at square one.

Your exposure would come when opportunity profits were lost on rising prices. Assume you sold a $400 call. A move above this level would mean your gold could be "called away" at $400 and you would sacrifice any profit above this price. Keep in mind that you can replace your inventory by paying the difference between your strike and cash gold. If you are nimble, your lost opportunity will be small.

Further variations on the theme involve selling different inside strikes while buying different outside strikes. This is almost the same as a butterfly, but the "body" consists of different put and call strikes. Assume gold is trading at $390. You would sell

F I G U R E 4–3

A Condor

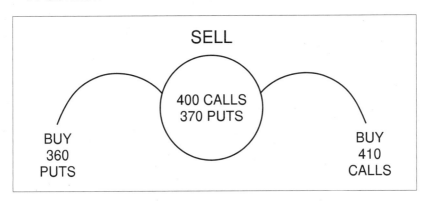

the 400 call and 370 put while buying the 410 call and 360 put (see Figure 4–3). The trade will yield a credit because options closer to the current futures price have higher premiums. If prices remain between the two inside options by expiration, you collect your premium. If prices rise above the 400 inside call, you make the amount of the price rise up to the 410 outside call while your puts become worthless. A breakout above 410 caps your profit at $10 plus your premium. This strategy is frequently called a "condor."

COMBINING FUTURES AND OPTIONS

In some cases, you will find a net positive transaction involving futures and options combinations. In the case of silver, anticipation and false breakouts created the perfect environment for selling options without underlying inventory. In August of 1996, I recommended selling December silver 525 calls and 500 puts for combined premiums of 25 cents. Although silver traded above the calls and below the puts, the transaction was lifted after premiums had deteriorated to below 10 cents. Exposure was confined to a move above $5.50 or below $4.75. In other words, either strike would need to be exceeded by the 25-cent premium collected on the transaction. By the middle of September, the 500 calls and puts were yielding a combined 30 cents. Although the call or put would be highly likely to be in the money by December expiration, the price would need to exceed $5.30 or fall below $4.70 before the transaction would begin losing on an expiration basis. Thus, if the price dipped to $4.75 on expiration, there would still be a 5-cent profit assuming all positions were properly liquidated. The silver contract represented 5,000 ounces. Therefore, every penny was worth $50. A 5-cent profit was $250. Margin on the transaction was as low as $1,000. Your gain was 25 percent. These are not hypothetical trades; all of these opportunities actually existed within the time frames mentioned.

Intracommodity Strategies

The unique aspect of new precious metals markets is the remarkable price stability. Trading ranges have been extremely reliable. Equally important, when prices for silver and gold did break technical support and resistance barriers, premiums became so rich that adverse price movements could be offset. In comparison, the metals markets of the 1970s were so reactionary that exposures were too great to use these strategies. In addition, liquid options did not exist. Some believe the very options strategies reviewed in this chapter have confined prices within ranges. Professional traders who implement selling strategies in calls and puts will try to trade futures into their ranges. Because many traders work off the same historical patterns, ranges can become self-fulfilling prophecies. Everyone wants to preserve the range.

Even before options, there were ways to earn money on inventories using futures. You may be familiar with the term *basis* used in commodity markets. The difference between the cash price and a futures contract price is the basis. There are also differences between consecutive expiration months called *intracommodity* spreads. For example, April gold will have a lower price than June, June will be lower than August, August lower than October, and so on. The basis and spread difference represent a cost of holding gold that includes an assumed storage charge, assay fee, insurance premium, and interest rate. In a normal market, the further the month is from the present time, the wider the spread or basis. This price difference will converge on the cash price as expiration approaches. Producers and consumers use futures to protect against adverse price movements. If you own gold and are afraid prices will fall, you could sell futures short. Any negative price movement yields a profit on a short sale. Suppose the current gold price is $450 per ounce in January. You notice February gold has a price of $455. There is a $5 difference. By selling short February gold, you automatically earn $5 more than the current selling price and you have locked in the $455 price.

What if prices go up? You have the gold to deliver and you have sacrificed the opportunity profit above $455. If gold remains static, the $5 spread will eventually shrink to zero and you have earned $5 in about one month on 100 ounces ($500 on $45,000 worth, or 1.1 percent). Calculated over twelve months, this process could earn 13.2 percent if each spread were uniform at 1.1 percent. In reality, the spread will closely reflect a short-term interest rate like a 90-day Treasury bill. The hedge income generated from consecutive short sales is likely to be low, but it is still income. The purpose of this strategy is to earn a modest return while protecting against disaster. Further, if call option premiums are low, you can finance call purchases from the hedge income. If a breakout materializes, you are long at the call strike and you profit from any bull market.

In the immediate aftermath of peak 1980 precious metals prices, investors were torn between holding silver and gold for security or buying Treasury notes and bonds for high yields. Spreads were below bond yields and traders found it comforting to buy futures on margin while investing the remaining cash in government securities. This allowed interest to accumulate on cash reserved for precious metals purchases. Unfortunately, gold prices declined and the futures positions lost money. However, the losses were the same as if the cash had been used to buy the actual gold or silver.

Intercommodity Spreads

Aside from intracommodity strategies, you can take advantage of intercommodity spreads. Historically, platinum prices exceed those of gold. However, there have been instances where the price difference between platinum and gold became narrow. The merging of the COMEX and NYMEX has allowed traders to economically "spread" the platinum group metals against gold and silver. *Spreads* involve the purchase and sale of commodities in anticipation of a change in the difference between prices. In the case of platinum versus gold, one would buy platinum and sell gold when the price difference became small or negative. Spreads are quoted with the "long leg" or buy side first. Therefore, a "platinum/gold spread" involves buying platinum and selling gold. If the spread were referred to as gold/platinum, you would be buying gold and selling platinum.

In theory, precious metals move in tandem. In practice, this has not been the case during the past several years. Fundamental forces affecting platinum are substantially different today because platinum is a highly industrial precious metal. The majority of platinum is used in catalytic converters and petroleum cracking. As the volume of automobiles increases, so does demand for platinum. As more refineries come on-line, platinum demand will grow. On the other hand, platinum is a resilient metal that is not actually consumed in its catalytic role. The metal used as a catalyst can be recycled. This simplistic view will be covered more fully in Chapter 8. For the purpose of justifying a platinum/gold strategy, it is important to understand that industrial demand for platinum coupled with limited supply tends to hold the platinum premium over gold.

A strategy of buying platinum and selling gold when the spread narrows to a $5 platinum premium and lifting the spread at $25 has worked well over time (see Figure 4–4). There were two instances when the spread went seriously negative. However, in all instances through 1996, platinum has recovered its premium over gold. Here, a careful review of the structural differences between platinum and gold must be continuous. As later chapters reveal, certain demographic patterns imply that gold requirements could accelerate during the next several decades. In particular, China and India could become major consumers for religious and cultural reasons. The key is to observe consumption patterns in both metals relative to supply. Although gold demand

F I G U R E 4–4

Platinum/gold spread. The price difference between gold and platinum (spread) offers unique profit potential.

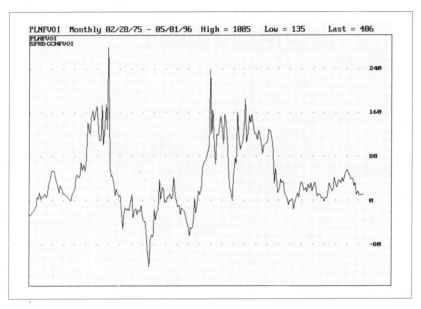

may have good prospects as wealth increases in China and India, there are huge central bank reserves that can act as a buffer.

Platinum has no such reserves. Based on this one structural difference, platinum prices can be more sensitive to shifting supply and demand fundamentals. Gold, on the other hand, is influenced by potential central bank or International Monetary Fund (IMF) sales.

Platinum's sister metal, palladium, also offers spread opportunities. Throughout the past decade, palladium has experienced the most relative strength, rising more than 100 percent in less than a decade. Technological advances in the use of palladium as a substitute for platinum in catalytic converters boosted the price ratio between these metals. The purchase of palladium against the sale of platinum has been a good longer-term strategy. However, platinum's popularity as an investment metal and in jewelry can cause positive swings against the palladium ratio. The palladium/platinum spread carries more risk than platinum/gold because the history is less stable and developments favoring palladium are recent. Investment accumulation of palladium is almost nonexistent relative to platinum, gold, and silver. Therefore, investors must rely on its industrial demand for significant price enhancements. It is interesting to note that only 20 percent more palladium was produced than platinum in 1994. Recent production growth appears to be stronger for palladium, with approximately 6.21 million ounces mined in 1995 compared with 4.89 million ounces of platinum. During 1996, the spread between platinum and palladium widened in favor of platinum because of a surplus differential. This is why the relationship between these metals may be too new for speculation.

As with gold, a cash platinum inventory lends itself to option writing. Platinum futures and options represent 50-ounce contracts in contrast with 100 ounces for gold and 5,000 ounces for silver. If platinum is trading at $420 per ounce, the total contract value is $21,000, whereas gold at $400 per ounce represents a contract value of $40,000 on 100 ounces. Platinum's smaller contract size makes it more manageable. In many cases, option premiums can be attractive. However, platinum has offered a less liquid market than gold and silver. Again, circumstances can quickly change. Commercialization of any new platinum-based technology can quickly shift investor interest toward platinum. Platinum can easily gain liquidity.

TECHNICAL ANALYSIS

Strategies designed to give precious metals a "yield" can be enhanced through certain timing mechanisms. You are probably familiar with technical analysis and chart interpretation. Since the development of high-speed, low-cost computers, technical analysis has gained enormous favor and respectability. Once viewed as hocus-pocus by the academic and investment establishment, technical analysis has virtually taken over from fundamental analysis as the tool of choice. The Random Walk theory that contends past performance cannot predict future events has been significantly discounted in our new computer age. There is sound evidence that certain technical market approaches work.

With this in mind, option strategies can be optimized by more accurate timing and pattern recognition. For example, there are new computer systems that apply human problem-solving logic to pattern recognition. These systems are called "neural networks" and have displayed uncanny accuracy in predicting market behavior. Although the jury is still out on neural network performance, scientists know that these powerful programs can tell investors the probability markets are in trending or trading range patterns. This can be extremely useful information for writing (selling) call options against metal inventories.

If you can know with a certain confidence that gold will remain within certain price boundaries, your timing of option strategies can be more accurate. Obviously, call premiums will be higher if the strike price is closer. Neural networks can measure the probability of a breakout based on certain market patterns, which may include an analysis of price momentum, open interest changes, and volume. In the past, the artful technical analysis practitioner would "eyeball" a chart and use intuition to determine "support" and "resistance" price levels. It is true that certain individuals seem to have a sixth sense for picking tops and bottoms, but for the average investor, mechanical systems and statistical tools are the next best thing to clairvoyance.

As the publisher of the daily COMMODEX® System, I am familiar with using technical analysis for accurate timing. COMMODEX was developed during the 1950s by my father, the late Edward B. Gotthelf. The system is designed to automatically trade commodities based on certain price forecasting formulae and trading rules. Although the system is sufficiently robust to have withstood the test of time, applications for this mechanical approach have changed with market dynamics. There were no options when the system was developed. COMMODEX provides buy and sell signals for futures contracts. Because options are derivatives of futures, the system can apply to new strategies. A buy signal for futures can translate into the purchase of an option, the sale of a put, or both. A sell signal can lead to the purchase of a put, sale of a call, or both. Then, you can apply the combinations of options and futures to buy and sell signals. COMMODEX is a "trend-following system." This means it looks for markets that are moving consecutively higher or lower on balance. If no price trend is recognized, COMMODEX remains "neutral" with no position. This is different from a "reversal system," which is always long or short, but never neutral.

When COMMODEX was introduced in 1959, neutral signals could not be traded. Today, neutral can be the basis for selling both calls and puts above and below the futures price. If the market remains trendless, the options will lose value and the investor can collect the premium as it deteriorates. This is particularly good for trading precious metals. Given the long "dry spells" when gold, silver, and the platinum group remain in ranges, it is comforting to know there is no technical basis for a breakout or bust. Whether you apply the COMMODEX system, moving average cross-overs, Relative Strength, stochastic indicators, Market Profile®, or a host of other technical tools is not important. The key is to use these tools in an integrated strategy for collecting revenue from the new precious markets.

INVESTMENT METHODS

The World Gold Council has published "A Guide to Investing in Gold." This informative pamphlet touches on traditional approaches without discussing strategies. The council highlights ten ways to invest:

- Bullion
- Bullion coins
- Numismatic coins
- Statement accounts
- Accumulation plans
- Mining shares
- Mutual funds
- Futures
- Options
- Forwards

Except for forwards, which require large financial commitments, these areas apply to individual investors and are available for silver, platinum, and palladium. Platinum and palladium have few, if any, numismatic coins because these metals were hardly used for coin of the realm. In addition, palladium does not have sufficient popularity for the development of statement accounts or accumulation plans. These facts aside, the ten investment methods can be broken into four categories:

- Physical holdings
- Custodial holdings
- Derivatives
- Equities

I consolidate these further into the traditional, progressive, and participatory. If you own coins or bullion, you're a *traditionalist*. If you trade futures and options, you are *progressive*. If you own equities, you are *participatory*, that is, involved in the rewards of production and distribution.

Strategically, there are times to own metal, times to trade progressively, and times to participate in equities. Further, all three have a measure of overlap in today's precious metals environment. This is to say that a precious metals advocate can justify owning metal or having a custodial account simply for insurance against disaster. A disaster favors physical metal over a custodial account because the investor cannot know the position any custodian like a bank or brokerage house might take during a panic. When all else fails, the investor would need coins or bars. There is a serious question as to whether anyone would be safe in a crisis of such proportions as to require a flight to gold and silver.

Leaving this philosophical question and intellectual exercise aside, nothing would be more secure than metal. If some technological breakthrough like cold fusion becomes a commercial reality, demand for palladium and platinum could be so explosive as to justify owning metal for fear of a complete market "lockout." Based on current palladium production and technology rumors, palladium prices could climb to $5,000 an ounce while remaining economically viable for supporting the cold fusion process. As little as a half ounce of palladium could power an entire home for thousands of years. If true, $5,000 an ounce might be a bargain. At the first hint of commercial feasibility, you and I would probably be locked out of the market. Yet, if we own ten, twenty, or a hundred ounces of palladium at prices ranging from $100 to $200, this modest investment can grow into a small fortune. There is no doubt you would be making a bet on unproven technology. But the gamble is worth the price for those who can afford the sacrifice. As of this writing, platinum was more than three times more expensive than palladium. This can place it out of range for some investors. Platinum does not play as critical a role in the hypothetical cold fusion process. This situation suggests the odds favor palladium for now.

As later chapters demonstrate, equities are the best precious metals "investments." When you own mining stocks, you participate in production and distribution. You make your gains the old-fashioned way—through earnings. In a reasonably stable stock market environment, stocks and mutual funds are sound and effective. In particular, gold stocks and mutual funds have the advantage of widening profit margins based on stable prices and falling production costs. Yes, the ratio between price and cost can fluctuate. Some companies will have better numbers than others. But the process of mining and selling gold, silver, platinum, and palladium in a free and open market should maintain better than average performance.

When trading equities, an investor must be aware of the general market environment. Even gold stocks can suffer during an overall collapse. When picking individual stocks, the investor must consider properties, location, management, technology, financial strength, political environment, and a string of other fundamental factors. Should one invest in a dedicated mine that specifically produces gold, silver, platinum, or palladium? Or should the investor look at a base metal producer that spins off large by-product precious metals production? What technology is in place? Are investors looking at deep shaft or strip mines? What are the ore grades and how much does the metal cost to refine? When later chapters review specific metals in greater detail, you will see how many considerations exist. Selection is a complex process.

If you choose a mutual fund, you should determine the management philosophy. Is it a "small cap" fund? Are choices highly speculative, or are investors investing in an established mix of companies? The most popular funds deal exclusively in gold stocks. There are international funds, country-specific funds, and sector-specific funds. Speculative or "venture funds" may invest in startup companies, partnerships, or even property rights. You can even seek out funds that specialize in mining technology stocks. The variety is almost endless.

I should point out that equities have associated options, too. Speculating in stocks can be linked to the general market environment, or the specific metal price trend. Understand that production costs are relatively fixed compared to product price fluctuations. Although that statement may appear obvious, rising metals will lead rising profit margins. Sometimes you might miss the move in physical metal but catch the reaction in subsequent stock movement. These relationships call for integrated strategies. In the old days, precious metals did not involve so many strategic considerations. Obviously, market structure has changed. It is now extremely complex.

It is unfortunate that so much of the promotion of gold, silver, and (to a lesser extent) platinum and palladium is based on an assumption of doom and gloom. There is an inherent tendency to link the need to invest in gold and silver with a pending hyperinflation or global monetary meltdown. The truth is no such disasters are required to inspire precious metals higher. Facts indicate that population patterns and general global wealth are the more likely motivators for these markets during the next several decades. Yes, inflation can be the catalyst for a new major bull market. Yes, a monetary crisis can drive people back to hard assets. Yes, a change in political atmosphere can ignite a panic. No, these are not the absolute requirements for rising precious metals prices.

CHAPTER 5

Price Action

Research associated with this book guided me to hundreds of sources. Throughout my investigations, I found the majority of readily available information came from individuals and organizations that were subjectively interested in promoting bullish prospects for precious metals. Facts and figures associated with precious metals are often obscured by an ever-continuing optimism about higher prices. During the mid-1990s, there was an increasing awareness among producers that their markets are elastic and price sensitive. As commodities, the higher the price, the more restricted the demand. The lower the price, the more affordable the metal. This contrasts with the theory that demand for precious metals can and does increase with price.

THE ROAD NOT TAKEN

Certainly, the buying frenzy of 1979–80 established a precedent for the positive correlation between rising prices and rising demand. Refer again to Figure 1–1 in Chapter 1 to examine the effect of a "herd mentality" on silver when prices make an extreme advance. However, the circumstances of a panic are not the same as those of a normal market. In reality, silver and gold had no identities. People simply did not understand how pricing should be correlated.

Price sensitivity became clear when industrial consumers screamed for alternatives to silver, gold, and platinum following the 1980 price peaks. From 1977 through 1984, gold and silver were "event driven." Prices would react to specific events with very little supply consideration. This extraneous performance correlation presented the incentive for users to seek alternatives. You may recall that Europe did not require catalytic converters on cars and trucks through the 1970s and 1980s. The surge in platinum prices played a strong role in their delay toward cleaner air. At the time pollution control was being examined, technology was at a fork in the road between "lean-burn" engines and the conventional catalytic converter. As platinum prices began retracing to reasonable levels, catalytic devices appeared more economical than implementing entirely new combustion technologies.

What would have happened if Europe adopted lean burn over catalysts? Considering the amount of platinum and palladium dedicated to automobiles and trucks, it is fair to say price margins for the platinum group metals would have been seriously challenged. With today's increasingly powerful computers, lean-burn technology is more feasible. Ignition, fuel/air mixture, fuel monitoring, suspension adjustment, and gear shifting can be more precisely controlled by tiny automobile "brains." Assuming manufacturers do not move to an entirely new power system, don't be surprised to find yourself driving a vehicle that operates more efficiently without the use of a catalytic device. Japan already has such cars.

As strange as it may seem, dynamic price histories for gold, silver, platinum, and palladium are extremely short. From a marketing perspective, none of these metals are mature. It is as though gold and silver were introduced as commodities in the 1970s. Platinum and palladium actually have more "product maturity." Yet even these metals have a brief price history. There is evidence platinum was used in ancient Egypt and by Native Americans. Whether they knew the distinction between platinum and silver is unknown. Certainly, platinum is a harder metal than silver and is more difficult to work. As an element, platinum was analyzed in the 1700s. However, commercial production was not feasible until the nineteenth century. This is an important consideration when one examines price patterns. With so little historical behavior to analyze, we cannot be sure of consistency. What may appear as a pattern or trend today can easily change tomorrow. This is why precious metals remain so interesting and exciting. The lack of dynamic pricing has hardly been raised as an issue. I believe it is one of the main issues! Incredible as it may sound, governments still maintain a market-independent "official price" for gold and silver. This suggests these markets are still not fully weaned from fixed pricing to dynamic pricing. Indeed, the subtle ties may never be completely broken.

Adding confusion to pricing fundamentals is the fact that so much metal is by-product. This means that costs are somewhat amorphous because they are derived from various allocation methods. For example, silver is produced as a by-product of copper, nickel, zinc, and other base metals. The primary manufacturing goal is mining the base metal. The consequential extraction of silver and other precious metals has limited direct cost, which is fractional compared with allocated costs. From an accounting standpoint, by-product metals should share in general overhead and capital allocation. But silver and gold would be there regardless of any allocation.

Given these facts, it is difficult to determine how low prices can sink before it is no longer economically feasible to produce precious metals. This is exactly why so many analysts and metals advisors were wrong when they predicted silver production would shut down if prices dipped below $6.50 per ounce. There was too much emphasis on dedicated silver mining and too little attention to by-product production. Silver mines *did* shut down. But their production was picked up by increases in other mining operations.

PRICE AND DEMAND

What is a realistic market price for gold and silver? The markets tell us. Suppose the average cost of an ounce of gold sinks to $50. Would the market price fall in tandem? Price behavior suggests gold and silver pricing is demand-skewed. This means that demand plays a more important role in determining value. It is a fact that the average cost of gold extraction has declined. It is a fact that demand has held gold's market price relatively steady from the mid-1980s forward. With this in mind, we can take a fresh look at precious metals pricing to derive a better perspective. How realistic are expectations for prices of $500, $750, and $1,000 per ounce of gold? What is the probability silver will soar to $25, $50, or more than $100? Will platinum rocket toward $1,000? Can palladium follow or lead? Examining price patterns cannot tell us what circumstance will eventually determine prices. However, we can judge volatility, sensitivity, stability, seasonality, cycles, and trends.

Our study of fundamentals for each metal will bring out pricing potential. You should have a sense of where supply and demand are going in the years ahead. Any attempt at long-range forecasting is guesswork, at best. However, my prediction that gold and silver would experience steady declines through the 1980s and 1990s proved correct in the face of dozens of contradicting forecasts. Everything from the fall of the Soviet Union to the new South African government to strikes in Chile and Peru was the basis for phantom bull markets. For investors following the advice of "experts," the road has been rough and frustrating. I have worked with people in the precious and base metals industry to formulate long-term marketing plans and hedge strategies. I cannot tell you how difficult it is to convince a major gold or silver producer that the price is going down, down, down! In some cases, I was fired, hired, and fired again! In all cases, my consulting services proved highly profitable for those willing to accept reality.

In my work in the precious metals area, I discovered the true meaning of "expert opinion" and "research study." At the investment level, they translate as "useless!" I read the most detailed reports on supply and demand and the most scientific forecasts from the most respected consulting groups. In almost all instances from 1985 forward to 1996, the bias was for higher prices. The very people who sponsored so much of this analysis and research were substantially responsible for price declines. The whole industry stood in amazement when silver prices broke down below $5 an ounce in 1990 and proceeded to test fifteen-year lows by 1991! It was the industry that continued selling into this market. Why was the downward spiral such a surprise? The structural change in silver production that shifted from primary to secondary production encouraged using this metal as a sacrificial lamb in support of other operations. Yet report after report indicated that supply was in serious trouble. In particular, the post-1987 stock market crash was supposed to tip the scales in favor of higher silver prices. There had already been a spike up in prices beginning in the second quarter of 1987 from approximately $5.50 to almost $10. The market was expected to follow this pattern as investors sought to shore up paper portfolios with hard assets.

In reality, the liquidity crunch associated with the crash caused hard asset liquidation to shore up paper. In some cases, metal was the only thing left to sell in order to raise cash to meet margin commitments. Although some may argue this logic comes with the benefit of 20/20 hindsight, writing was on the wall immediately after equities hit bottom. None of the metals were responsive. The heaviest campaigns to promote silver and gold failed to raise investor interest.

This is important because investors hold the "swing demand." Investors are the unknown factor that can instantly change. Investors can absorb or expunge metal without regard for industrial circumstances. Investors drove prices to extremes in 1979–80. Investors abandoned metals in favor of paper assets through the 1980s.

Factors Affecting Price

It is reasonable to assume that investors will regain confidence in precious metals only if there is a significant change in market environment. Even if demand from Third World nations accelerates, the price rise must be coupled with some fundamental alteration in investor psychology. This comes with two types of events. First, a general currency devaluation; inflation. Second, a confidence crisis. Absent these two developments, investor interest is likely to be related to interim ups and downs. Participation in the market will continue to be sporadic.

F I G U R E   5–1

Silver Price in Actual and 1987 Dollars

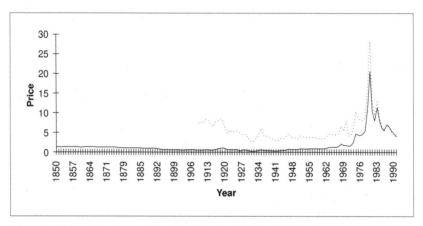

Source: Adapted from table in *Bureau of Mines Minerals Yearbook*, 1992, pp. 157–158.

Having been confined to fixed prices during the time of monetary linkage, gold and silver values can be measured only in terms of a purchasing standard. Figure 5–1 plots the actual silver price against a price in 1987-indexed U.S. dollars from the period 1850 through 1991.

It is immediately apparent that silver's cash price was virtually flat through 1960. For more than a century of consecutive years, the price hardly budged. With the exception of the 1979–80 price hike, silver prices were contained at less than $10 per ounce. From 1910 through 1965, the relative value of silver in 1987 dollars was declining. After the shock of 1979–80, silver returned to its range which averaged around $5.89. The apparent secular trend continued down from 1980 through 1996. The fact that silver prices display such a poor performance on an inflation-adjusted basis is intriguing because most individuals believe silver prices should track the price index. Silver was as cheap in 1996 as it was in 1976 without an inflation adjustment. Thus, through twenty years of constantly rising prices, silver failed to keep up with inflation.

What does this say about silver? It should be clear that this metal has been neither an inflation hedge nor a good investment. Any long-term silver hoarding has provided a negative return on an adjusted and nonadjusted basis. Silver, in effect, is "just a commodity" and it is typically responsive to supply and demand relationships. Therefore, the most important emphasis for this market must be consumption and production. Unless there is an unexpected and dramatic structural change in silver, this is not a metal to buy and hold. Unfortunately, too few investors take the time to actually examine silver's long-term price history. When you do, you must ask yourself, "Why would this metal make a good long-term investment?"

Short- versus Long-Term Prospects

Refer again to Figure 5–1, and you can be the judge. Does the price pattern look encouraging to you? This is an important perspective because the sales pitch for silver relies on a narrow slice of history—from 1974 through 1984. You are supposed to believe what all investors see happening—that silver will return to its most lofty levels. If you examine silver's economics as presently structured, such a price rise is not industrially feasible because it would severely stress commercial applications. At $50 per ounce, the price for silver-based technology would rise beyond elasticity. Would you pay $25 for a roll of 35mm color film? Silver solders, electronic contacts, pastes, alloys, mirrors, purifiers, and other products would be priced out of their markets. At the very least, there would be strong financial incentives to find alternatives.

Based on price behavior through 1996, there appears to be more of a chance prices will deteriorate than advance over the longer term. To be sure, silver could pop up to $6, $8, and $10 during market dislocations. But price analysis points toward real values as low as $2 or $1.50. If silver can break below the $2 barrier, there is a strong possibility it can return as a monetary metal. Does this sound strange? The lower the price, the greater the incentive to use silver as coinage. Silver coins accomplish two goals. First, silver gives the appearance of value. Second, at low prices, silver is as good as any other metal! Governments would be slow to adopt silver coinage because there is always a fear that some shortage will drive prices up. At any time, industrial consumption may rise. Unless there is some way to control prices, there is too much exposure to arbitrage.

American mints experienced such problems with copper pennies when market value exceeded face value. There was an incentive for the public to hoard pennies, which reduced supplies in circulation. This is a problem treasuries will continue to face as industrial demand for any form of metal raises market value beyond a practical face value. At some stage, plastic may be the only alternative. Consider that plastic coins can be encoded to prevent counterfeiting. Plastic is lightweight and durable. It is unlikely there would ever be an incentive to hoard or melt down plastic coins. Other practical alternatives might be steel and aluminum.

Futurists tell us the entire coinage scenario is completely wrong. Eventually, we will have no need for money because our transactions will be conducted using handprints, fingerprints, voice recognition, or some other high-tech approach. In response to this, I would advise anyone to hide some gold. You never know when you may need it!

SILVER

Figure 5–2 illustrates silver price behavior from 1968 through 1972, from 1975 through 1977, and from 1990 through the first four months of 1996. The figure reveals that silver has a tendency to consolidate into narrow trading ranges over extended periods of between three and five years. With the exception of the 1968–72 consolidation, prices settled within similar ranges around $5 per ounce. Given a span of approximately three decades, the observations suggest silver has a natural equilibrium around the $5 level. Any movement significantly above $5 should eventually return, whereas any dip below that price should result in a recovery. This assumption is based on consistent fundamentals. If there were a discovery that silver could cure cancer or purify the world's water supply, the equilibrium level could be raised. By the same token,

F I G U R E 5–2

Silver Prices 1968–72 (top), 1975–77 (middle), and
1990–96 Four Months (bottom)

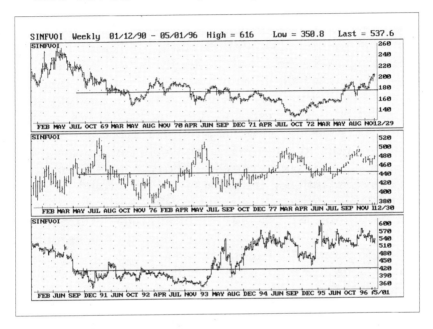

if digital photography completely displaces conventional film, the
equilibrium price could find a lower level. However, we can
expect the same price behavior whether silver finds a higher or
lower consolidation range.

This steady price behavior probably carries over from the
time when silver prices were fixed. Perhaps it is habitual. There
was a great deal of conjecture throughout the amazing price spiral
of the late 1970s. This event was correlated with two developments. There was the famous attempt by the Hunt brothers of
Texas to "corner" the silver market. The Hunts tried to control
sufficient supplies to manipulate prices. The Hunts were not alone
in this wild speculation. As oil producers, the Hunts formed an
alliance with Middle East interests and planned to reestablish
silver as a monetary instrument. Some may recall that crude oil
was being rapidly devalued by dollar inflation during this time.

Because oil was priced in U.S. dollars, producers were concerned that they were not receiving payment in a stable form. Hence, the focus on silver.

Adding to this was the inflation itself. Investors joined in the silver bonanza because currency was considered in crisis. What would have happened if the Hunts had succeeded in their plan? History implies that prices would have settled back into a trading range. There is no indication prices would have moved appreciably above the 1980 top of just under $45 per ounce. Thereafter, the Hunts as well as the investing world would have been surprised to find silver seeking its normal levels. This is because Western Europe, the United States, and Japan would have implemented the same plans to stabilize currencies and economies. Eventually, confidence in currency, silver-backed or not, would have returned. While the high price might have been extended, silver's inherent price behavior should have forced a return to the $5 level.

For those inclined to speculate in silver, the ratios are obvious. At $5 per ounce, the most you can lose is $5. Clearly, this is theoretical because it is impossible to think that silver would be thrown into the streets. There is a practical downside lurking around $1 to $1.50. Below these prices, the process of extraction, assay, transportation, and storage could be adversely affected. If you must own this metal, levels of $5 or less represent a "comfort zone." Buying metal above the comfort zone increases risk and exposure. Certainly, you might trade a price reaction. Caution is in order when purchasers consider an accumulation program.

Bull Markets

When prices do break out into a major bull trend, history shows a relatively short duration: approximately one year. The bull market of the late 1970s began in 1978 with a move above $5 (see Figure 5–3). Prices reached only $6.25 by 1979. From 1979 to January 1980, prices reached almost $45. Within two months, silver retraced below $11.25. Technically, silver displayed a classic pattern. Following the 1980 plunge, prices recovered approximately half the distance from top to bottom. This follows a 50 percent retracement rule. By 1982, prices reached back down to

F I G U R E 5–3

The beginning of a bull market in the late 1970s is reflected in silver prices here.

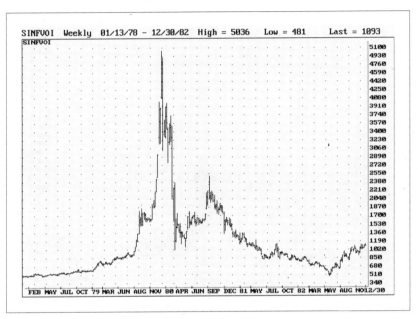

the "good old" $5 level. From July 1982 to February 1983, silver staged another rally to a high of $15. Within thirty months, it was back down to $5 (see Figure 5–4).

Interim Action

Regardless of silver's long-term price prospects, interim movements have been exciting and significant. A jump from $5 per ounce to $6 is a 20 percent increase. When translated into profit potential in the futures or options market, leverage multiplies profitability by as much as 100 percent. Assuming a silver margin of $1,000 per futures contract, a $1 gain represents a $5,000 profit for a 500 percent return. Examine yearly ranges for silver from 1981 through 1995 as shown in Table 5–1.

FIGURE 5–4

The end of the bull market is also reflected in silver
prices, which returned to the $5 per ounce level.

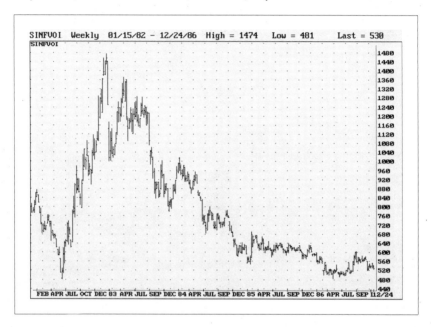

SINFVOI   Weekly   01/15/82 – 12/24/86   High = 1474   Low = 481   Last = 530

The smallest range of 70 cents occurred in 1992. Even this lack
of movement represents a $3,500 fluctuation in contract value.
Obviously, your profit opportunity would depend on the consistency with which silver moved from high to low coupled with
your transaction timing. An examination of silver price movements from 1981 through 1995 as shown in Figure 5–5 reveals
good trending tendencies and reasonable seasonal consistency.

Nine of the fifteen years exhibited seasonal downtrends
within the first quarter. The second quarter provides strength,
whereas the last quarter begins the weakness that is carried into
the first quarter. Of course, these generalizations are not the rule.
Certainly, 1982 provided a strong exception, with prices rallying
into 1983. Strategically, investors' objective is to formulate trading
programs that can take advantage of annual volatility. Interest-

T A B L E 5–1

Yearly Price Ranges for Silver

Year	High	Low	Range
1981	1,653	797	856
1982	1,130	481	649
1983	1,474	838	636
1984	1,753	624	1,129
1985	1,230	570	660
1986	799	503	296
1987	1,015	544	471
1988	1,089	598	491
1989	886	508	378
1990	643	393	250
1991	455	351	104
1992	433	363	70
1993	544	352	192
1994	579	453	126
1995	616	434	182

Note: 1984–90 are for December futures, whereas all other years are for a synthetic continuation contract.

ingly, a thirty-day moving average was applied to prices as a method for "deseasonalizing" price data. The relatively long interim price trends suggest you can approach this market with a seasonal filter. This simple method seems to generate handsome profits over most of the fifiteen-year period.

When confronted with silver's price behavior, the application of a penetration factor or a longer average may yield better results because intermittent crossings of price with the average are eliminated or minimized. Experience shows that a penetration factor can be more efficient because longer moving averages have a tendency to give back too much profit in a fast-moving market. Equally important, silver's propensity to remain in wide trading ranges supports strategies using options as previously covered. It is fair to say that silver is not like a good company stock. You cannot "buy and hold."

F I G U R E 5–5

Silver Price Movements, 1981 through 1995

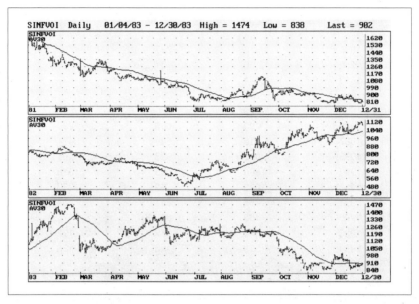

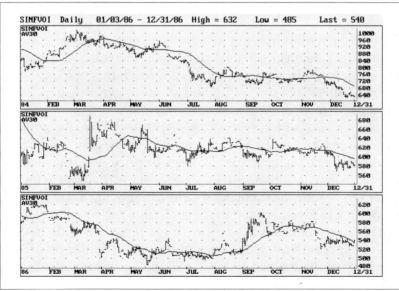

FIGURE 5–5

Continued

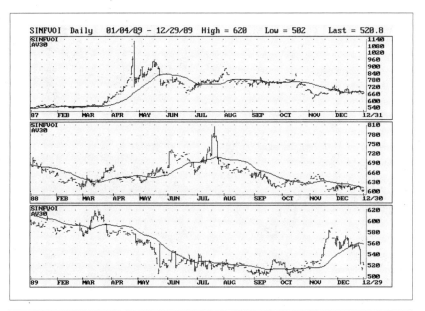

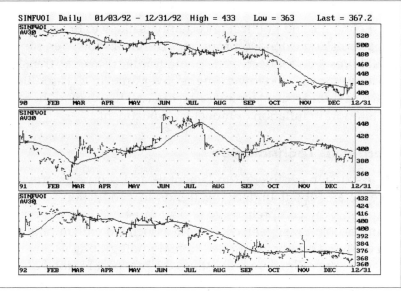

F I G U R E   5-5

Concluded

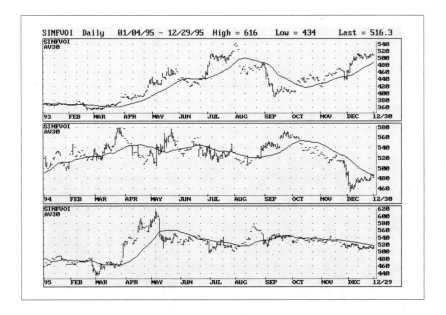

Economic and political uncertainty is likely to present cyclical patterns and extended profit opportunities. However, fundamental prospects for decreasing photographic usage can translate into lower "lows" and lower "highs" over time. In all cases, there must be a sound reason for investing in silver that extends beyond any temporary inflation or monetary adjustment.

Alternative Technologies

The discussion of silver's fundamentals and prospects provides more details about underlying trends in production and consumption. Any comprehensive review must evaluate the potential impact of new silver technologies associated with mining and usage. I have briefly mentioned digital photography as an alternative to silver film. How realistic is the prospect for total digital substitution? If digital does displace film, how much silver consumption will it impact?

Can other technologies pick up where photography leaves off? What about silver batteries? silver water purification systems? silver memory devices? These are some impressive technologies that can employ increasing amounts of silver in years ahead. I will explore the possibilities later.

GOLD

If you haven't guessed by now, I'll tell you. I really do love gold. I said it at the beginning of this text. My personal affinity for this metal pains me when I am forced to take an objective view concluding gold has not been a good investment. I confess the coins and bars I keep tucked safely away defy my better judgment. I admit that I have told others to divest or not to invest when I refuse to part with my personal stash. Emotions aside, Figure 5–6 plots gold prices in fixed dollars and indexed to 1987 dollars. From 1900 through the post-World War I recovery, gold's purchasing parity declined as measured against 1987 dollars. The pronounced parity spike following the 1929 stock market crash reflects the extraordinary deflation of the Great Depression. In reality, this was gold's finest hour. Its "real value" as a function of buying power reached the highest levels of the twentieth century. (Of course, we must keep in mind that gold's price was fixed.)

It is interesting to note that gold's value during the Great Depression surprises many investors. Consider that the gold price was still fixed; the dollar was still linked. Gold circulated as money. With all these constraints in place, the massive deflation drove gold values to pre-1900 highs. This should tell you something about owning gold. Although the consensus is that gold is an inflation hedge, it is really a deflationary asset. Consider the average gold price from legalization in 1975 through 1995 as illustrated in Figure 5–7.

We certainly know inflation continued from 1980 forward. If, indeed, gold provided an inflation hedge, why did the 20-year average remain at approximately 40 percent of the 1980 high average? Gold's purchasing parity adjusted for inflation actually declined. The 1980 high was, in fact, an overreaction relative to the inflation of 1975 through 1979. Many analysts attribute this to

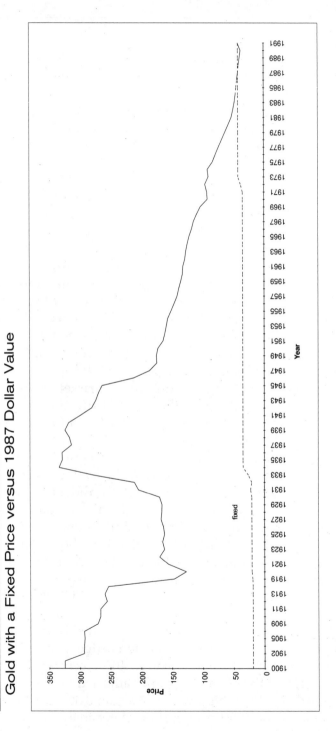

F I G U R E 5-6

Gold with a Fixed Price versus 1987 Dollar Value

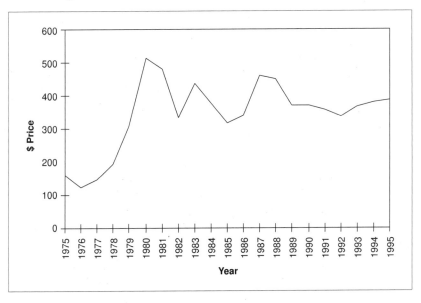

Average Cash Gold Price

a more powerful correlation to oil prices during that period. Therefore, it stands to reason that gold would seek a more realistic level on a true inflation-adjusted basis. The crossover was approximately 1983. Thereafter, gold prices still declined.

In 1990, I wrote an article for a precious metals company on the virtues of owning gold. In keeping with objectivity, I pointed out poor price performance and the lack of "investment return." The audience for the article was a group of hard-asset buyers who wanted to believe gold represented a safe financial haven. Based on the data, I reported that gold would be the asset of choice during a monetary realignment. We are all familiar with the concept of turning in currency on a formula. For example, the U.S. government might issue a "new" one dollar bill requiring the exchange of five old one dollar bills. The exchange formula is five-for-one. Unlike a genuine deflation, an exchange of old for new is a realignment. Because it is unlikely all prices will adjust to an exact formula, gold can act as a standard until prices seek new levels after the exchange.

Prices and Hoarding

As previously mentioned, gold is unlike any of its sister precious metals because it is almost entirely hoarded rather than consumed. Some may say this makes price analysis easier. I would disagree. With silver, platinum, and palladium, investors can attempt to measure supply and demand. With gold, investors face duality in supply and demand. Pricing is based on a combination of new gold and divested gold. Assuming no potential for divestiture, gold prices could be judged in the same manner as wheat or copper. Simply examine sources and output for each period compared against usage.

Alas, dynamics are not so simple. At any moment, the "instant" gold supply can double, triple, or increase tenfold. Obviously, central banks can sell reserves. Private hoards can be liquidated. Extreme crisis can drive gold into and out of the market. Extreme tranquility can produce a similar effect. Therefore, gold represents the ultimate financial game of chess. It is an environmental, political, and economic instrument that is unlikely to fade from the investment forum.

Figure 5–8 plots the Dow Jones Futures Index from October 31, 1933, through the end of 1981 as an illustration of how raw commodity prices responded from the Great Depression through the Great Inflation. The index is calculated on an average between 1924 and 1926 equaling 100. Although a futures price index does not directly consider labor, capital, and other important inputs affecting inflation, commodity prices generally respond during inflationary, deflationary, and stable periods. Note that the post-Depression recovery clashed with commodity shortages, which resulted in a general commodity inflation. This increase was accelerated by World War II, which imposed rationing to curb extraordinary price spirals. Once the war economy settled down, commodity prices remained virtually flat from 1955 through 1970.

FIGURE 5-8

The Dow Jones Futures Index responses to the economy from the Great Depression through the Great Inflation.

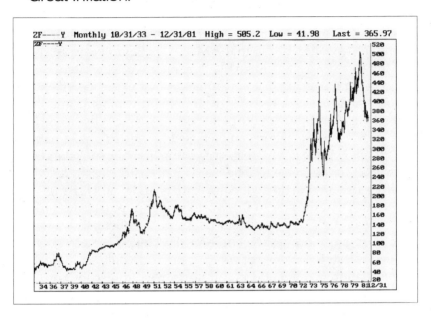

Of course, gold bugs will say that this stability was the result of Bretton Woods and the global adherence to gold. This does not explain why commodity prices shot up in 1971—before the gold standard was abandoned.

Commodity price action was linked to a series of natural, political, and economic events. Yes, there was a food crisis in 1971 that extended through 1973. Earlier I mentioned the corn leaf blight and subsequent Russian crop failures. Underpinning these natural price events was the rapid rebuilding of Europe and industrialization of Japan following World War II. There was a time in the late 1960s and early 1970s when "Made in Japan" was synonymous with "cheap" and poor quality. Americans bought a Japanese-made car when they could not afford anything else. Postwar Japan was not on a par with other "industrial countries." It did not take long for Japan to change this situation.

In the process of building industrial capacity and a unique process-driven economy, Japan exerted structural pressures on raw material prices, energy, and labor. The world had to keep up with Japan's accelerating ability to convert raw materials into finished products. At the same time, Germany was building its capacity and image whereby Americans moved from their focus on the Volkswagen Beetle to the Mercedes Benz coupe. In short, half the world was building wealth at an increasing rate.

One of the most popular campaign slogans echoed from the Nixon years forward by U.S. presidential incumbents and challengers has been, "Are you better off now than you were four years ago?" This question can be posed to industrialized nations in general. Has wealth increased as a function of living standards from 1933 to the present? The last U.S. Census clearly reveals a positive answer. Further, global wealth is undeniably rising. Any suggestion that the size of the world's poor population is indicative of negative wealth expansion is spurious. Liberals' arguments that there are more poor people in the United States, Canada, Mexico, Western Europe, or other regions are only an indication of population growth and nonuniform wealth distribution. The global standard of living is rising at an increasing rate as the direct result of increasing wealth.

Increasing wealth creates its own economic and monetary structural change. Wealth leads to demand. Demand leads to production. The inherent lack of synchronization between demand and production correlates with inflation and deflation. Technology and capacity caught up with wealth during the twenty years preceding the end of the twentieth century. Yet the very structural change that caused inflationary pressures during the 1970s could repeat as the Third World gains first-class status over time. Consider the comparison in terms of gold prices and commodities as illustrated in Figure 5–9.

Although an imperfect correlation, the link is clear here between the substantial breakout in gold and the steady rise in the commodity price index. It is interesting to note that gold was sleeping from 1975 through 1976 despite the pronounced jump in commodity prices. In fairness to gold, consider that prices jumped from the official price of $42.22 an ounce to more than $200 when

F I G U R E 5-9

Commodity Price Index 1975-81 (top) Compared
with Gold Prices 1975-81 (bottom)

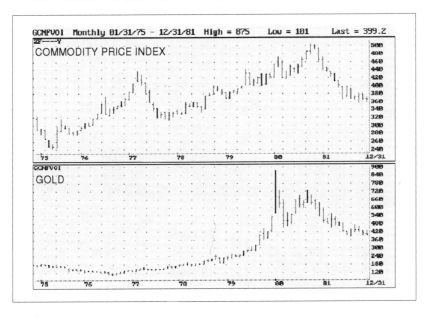

trading began on December 31, 1974. One could argue that this
473 percent climb reflected the Russian wheat deal and Arab Oil
Embargo. But how can this trend explain the lack of performance
during the next two years? The fact is that inflation alone was not
sufficient to excite precious metals. The ultimate requirement was
a monetary confidence crisis.

Seasonal Pricing

Lacking such a crisis, gold price action is the same as that of silver
with a slight twist. Gold's "unofficial role" as a reserve asset
buffers reactions to changing supply and demand fundamentals.
Regardless of this fact, gold as a commodity exhibits distinct price
patterns to use for speculation. Figure 5-10 presents a year-by-
year price history from 1975 through 1995. A monthly moving
average was applied for seasonal price smoothing. The years 1976

F I G U R E 5–10

Gold Prices 1975–95

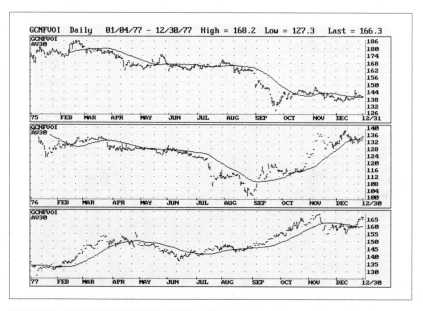

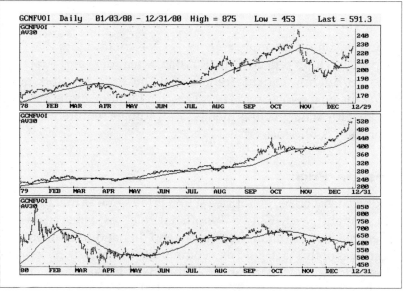

F I G U R E   5–10

Continued

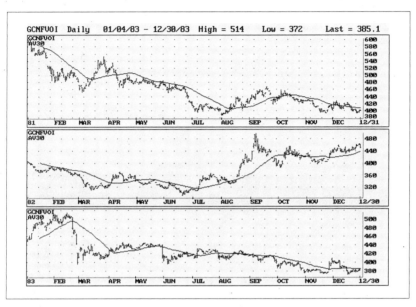

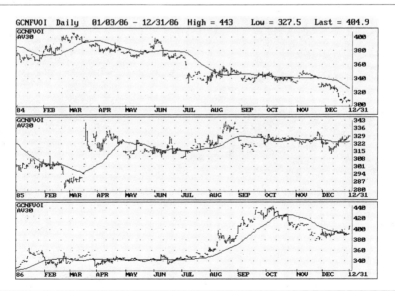

F I G U R E 5-10

Continued

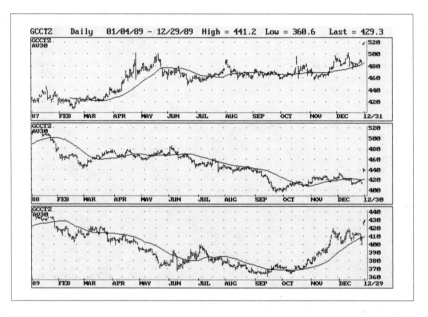

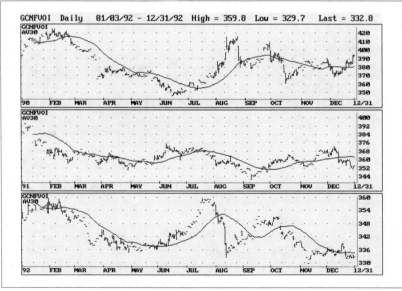

F I G U R E 5–10

Concluded

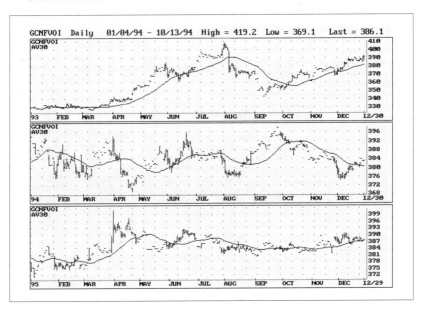

through 1982, 1986, and 1990 through 1994 show a tendency for gold to rally into the fourth quarter. With less consistency, gold sells off into the first quarter. This seasonal pattern has been correlated with the fourth-quarter holidays. Surveys show jewelry fabricators begin accumulating inventory toward the end of August. Demand increases through October. By November, goods are manufactured and shipped. Any excess inventory is liquidated during the first quarter of the following year.

Without the benefit of fundamental interpretation, Moore Research Center, Inc., of Eugene, Oregon, conducted technical research that determined the best time to sell gold futures was toward the end of January. This coincides with peak inventory liquidation and a slowdown in forward purchasing activity. The greatest profit potentials from short sales occur between mid-February and mid-March. Interestingly, the most significant interruptions in gold's seasonal tendencies came when central banks sold

F I G U R E   5–11

When indexed against dollar purchasing power,
gold's price can be normalized to show stable value
from 1985 through 1995.

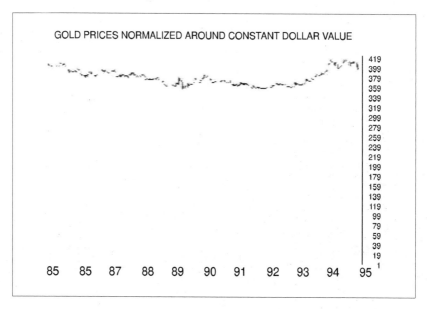

GOLD PRICES NORMALIZED AROUND CONSTANT DOLLAR VALUE

off reserves. This is extremely important to keep in mind as
investors develop their trading strategy. The real danger in trading gold comes from political uncertainty.

As central banks change their political outlooks for gold,
seasonal patterns can be disturbed. Any trading plan that seeks to
use seasonal patterns must keep a careful watch for untimely
central bank sales.

When we statistically "normalize" gold prices from 1989
through 1995 around constant U.S. dollars, we see an interesting
pattern suggesting that toward the later half of the 1990s, gold
actually increased in purchasing value despite its obvious decline
in dollar parity. As a parallel, recall that gold purchasing value
increased during the Great Depression. This was a deflationary
period. If the technical indicators are correct, steady gold values
from 1989 forward tell us Americans had balanced economic

growth against the money supply. We can also conclude that the fall in gold prices during 1995–96 was offset by a deflationary increase in purchasing parity. Because the price is recorded in U.S. dollars, we know that "disinflation" was accurately reflected by the gold market. Consider Figure 5–11, which plots the normalized gold price.

By indulging in broad hypotheticals, a case can be made for an economic shift that establishes new rules for today's economic environment. Assuming governments maintain control over our perceptions, technological progress plays catch-up with economic inadequacies. It is becoming less expensive to produce, communicate, track, control, manage, and entertain. This is an anti-inflation environment. If, in fact, we have created a fundamental change in the cost-push spiral, gold value will sustain any realignment. The technical forecast stands like the Rock of Gibraltar. There is no better constant than gold.

PLATINUM AND PALLADIUM

From the constant of gold and the speculative swings of silver, platinum and palladium offer a different twist to the precious metals complex. Because neither platinum nor palladium has played any monetary role, price analysis can be simplified. Although there is a modest amount of hoarding, the bulk of these metals is used for industrial purposes. This distills analysis down to basic supply and demand. We have little concern over the impact of "free stocks"—inventory similar to gold and silver held by central banks and monetary agencies. As covered in subsequent chapters, the "platinum group" metals have unique properties that are vital in particular industries. Aside from well-known requirements for automotive catalytic converters, there are extremely important applications in chemical processing and manufacturing for which no substitutes appear on the horizon.

Price Action

As a direct consequence of the industrial demand and consumption of platinum group metals, we see a well-defined "secular

Platinum Experiences Higher Lows to Indicate a
"Secular" Trend

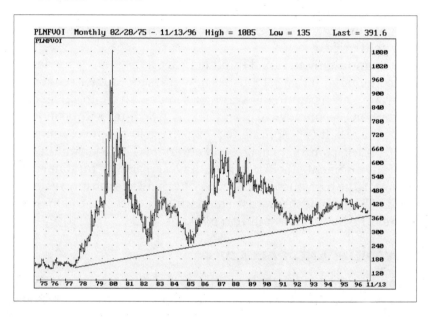

PLNFVOI   Monthly 02/28/75 - 11/13/96   High = 1085   Low = 135   Last = 391.6

trend" for platinum prices as reflected by Figure 5–12. I am
confident price action is primarily linked to the development and
widespread adoption of anti-pollution devices in most of the
developed countries. From 1975 through 1978, prices traded in a
narrow range between $135 and $180 per ounce. The inflation-
driven breakout in 1979–80 clouded the picture to some extent
because the price spike is not related to supply/demand fundamentals. Europe did not adopt catalysts until the late 1980s.

From late 1977 through 1996, platinum prices increased from
approximately $135 to $400. This represents a 196 percent increase
in nineteen years, for an average increase of 10.32 percent per year.
Even with an inflation adjustment, demand has pushed platinum
steadily higher. Although platinum's price performance as an
"investment" compared poorly with the Dow Industrial Average,
S&P 500, and other market indices during the late 1980s and 1990s,

stock market performance did not exceed a straight line average annual return of 15 percent during the 1970s and early 1980s.

Price Cycles

In conclusion, underlying demand fundamentals favor rising platinum prices providing there is no structural change adversely impacting its environment. A severe economic downturn might affect auto sales and, in turn, platinum demand. But, you can rest assured that stocks would encounter more adversity if such a severe recession occurred. Figure 5–13 clearly warns us that platinum is susceptible to multiyear cyclical behavior. The first price cycle of the 1980s began in 1978 and ended in 1982: four years. The next cycle was from 1982 to 1985: three years. The years 1985 to

F I G U R E 5–13

Cyclical Behavior of Platinum in Multiple Years

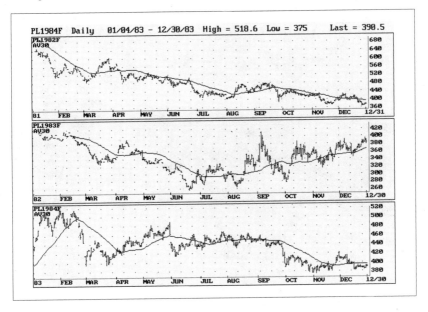

F I G U R E 5–13

Continued

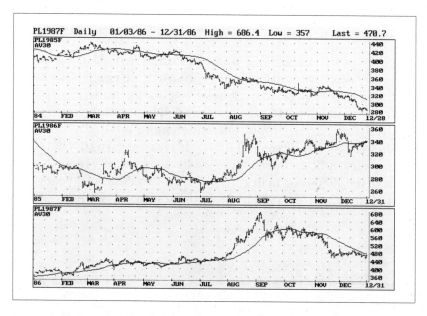

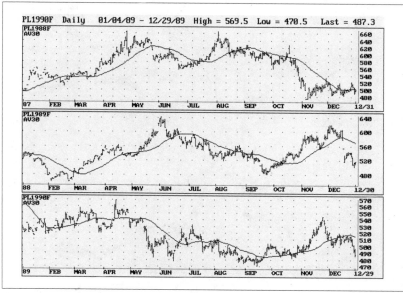

F I G U R E 5–13

Concluded

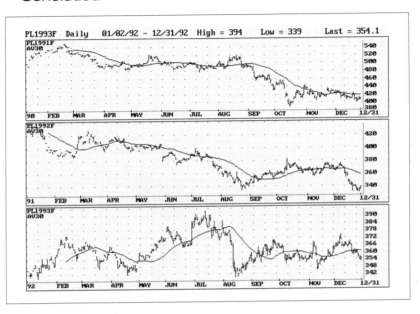

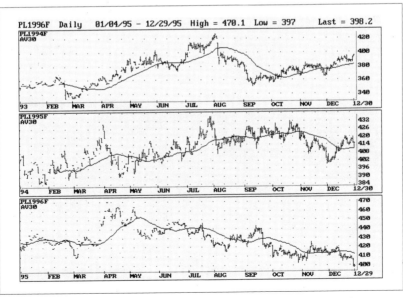

1991 marked the next cycle of four years, and from 1992 through 1996 there was a less dramatic four-year rise and fall.

Most industry information comes from two sources. The Platinum Guild is the primary industry group operating in the same way as the Gold and Silver Institutes. Then, Johnson Matthey, PCL, produces the annual *Platinum Report* with quarterly updates. These reports are similar to Goldfields, Ltd.'s *Gold Report.* Because industry-related literature is produced on a current basis looking forward, there is little retrospective coverage addressing the price cycle over the last three decades.

There is a strong link between platinum and crude oil, so several analysts believe their price action is dependent. Yet, a quick look at crude oil from 1983 through 1996 in Figure 5–14 indicates significantly different price action.

Cyclical crude oil action is more erratic, with no correlation between platinum peaks and troughs. Looking behind the scenes,

F I G U R E 5–14

Crude Oil Prices 1983–96 Near Contract Basis

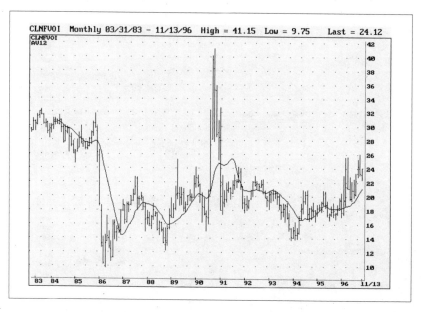

platinum's price action has been primarily related to politics. The two largest producers have been South Africa and members of the Commonwealth of Independent States (formerly known as the Soviet Union); both were prone to political turmoil and experienced major political transitions during the 1980s and 1990s. Both were involved in reformulating labor forces. Thus, price cycles can be statistically linked to developments within these producing countries.

The historical perspective revealed by news articles dating from 1980 to 1995 suggests interim platinum price movements were more supply-sensitive than demand-correlated. This is because platinum consumption patterns have been relatively steady and reasonably correlated with automotive, chemical, and energy industries. Simply put, a burst in platinum demand is not likely considering the complexion of industrial users. I would not rule out a speculative frenzy; however, such a development would probably stem from action in gold, silver, or totally new and dramatic technology. Here are major reasons for arguing the case for stability:

- Platinum is far less liquid than are gold and silver. Participation lacks diversity. The number of speculators is relatively small and their ability to swing prices has been questionable.

- Several industry analysts have called attention to the fact that the total quantity of platinum mined between 1995 and 1996 approximated 11 million ounces. Even at a high price of $400 an ounce, the total value of annual output comes to less than $2.5 billion. In effect, a speculator would be capable of accumulating a substantial quantity of this highly strategic metal with little capital. Assuming the use of futures or options, as little as $5 million could tie up 20 percent of deliverable supplies on a leveraged basis.

Platinum has been sensitive to real and rumored supply disruption. Because there is no easily mobilized platinum reserve, production closely tracks consumption. A key platinum characteristic that may mimic a "reserve" is derived from the metal's resilience. As a catalyst, platinum facilitates chemical reactions rather than being consumed by their processes. Although the metal's efficiency can deteriorate within a catalytic device, generally, most is recoverable. Assuming the domestic car "fleet" in the United States has an average age of seven years, recovered platinum should follow a somewhat muted seven-year or 3.5-year cycle. In addition to auto and truck catalytic converters, platinum is also recoverable from chemical plants and oil refineries. As an increasing amount of platinum is reprocessed, the industry has a propensity for an "industrial hoard." The more efficient the recovery process, the less new platinum is required to supplement scrap.

Seasonally, three out of fifteen years display a pronounced July–August rally followed by a total retracement. In 1986, 1987, 1988, 1993, 1994, and 1995, there was a tendency to rally into the first quarter. In 1981, 1982, 1984, 1990, and 1991, prices took a downward track in the first half, suggesting platinum does not display a strong seasonal pattern. Indeed, platinum prices appeared to follow automobile and light truck sales. Thus, longer-term forecasting tracked demand, whereas price events like "spikes" were highly correlated with labor unrest or political developments in South Africa and Russia. The thirty-day moving average smoothes price action sufficiently to indicate that "buy-and-hold" or "sell-and-hold" tactics work for long-term technical trading. Overall price trends have sufficient duration and distance to profitably accommodate this trading strategy. Unfortunately, we live in fast times with anxious expectations. Few individuals are willing to adhere to long-term trading using moving averages of thirty days or more. Today, it is almost unconscionable to hold a position in excess of a few weeks, let alone several months. Yet the charts clearly indicate that most years would have yielded handsome returns using long-term technical "filters."

In 1987 I conducted a study to determine where platinum prices were heading over the next ten years. Based on cyclical indications and patterns in the automotive/truck industry, my projections called for two events that proved remarkably accurate. First, I determined platinum would probably retrace its 1985–87 price rise from $240 to $660 by at least 50 percent. This would return prices to approximately $450. Indeed, prices declined to $450 and below to make a consolidation between 1991 and 1993 at around $360. My second conclusion was that prices would become less volatile as retired cars and trucks began to feed the scrap market. I based this on the fact that catalytic converters were introduced in the mid-1970s. Using turnover estimates, it seemed the first significant recycled platinum would begin to feed the market by 1985 and build thereafter. Platinum recycling would create a revolving door whereby scrap would increase overall supplies on a continuous basis. By 1988, recovered platinum accounted for 12 percent of the amount used for autocatalysts. Within five years, it had risen to 16.4 percent with an acceleration in 1994 and 1995. By the following year, it reached 17 percent. These figures as reported by Johnson Matthey, PLC, may be understated because they concentrate on autocatalysts. Considerable recycling also takes place in the petroleum industry where peak demand reached 150,000 ounces in 1991 and declined to 90,000 ounces by 1994. Recognizing these patterns, I believed platinum price action would calm in the absence of any extraordinary events.

It is possible that platinum's less volatile personality from 1991 forward through 1996 was a coincidence. As I will point out in reviewing fundamentals, other areas of consumption were growing to balance against recovered supplies. Yet I am convinced that the actual picture may not be properly represented in the statistics. In my opinion, recycled platinum as well as industrial inventories are underreported for strategic purposes. Depending on the rate of future recovery and recycling, supply disruptions will have less impact on prices because industrial users will have buffer stocks.

Palladium, on the other hand, is a new and different animal. Palladium's price movement has been highly correlated with technological advances that significantly increased industrial demand within a short period. This had a dual impact on the "platinum group" because the positive effect on palladium exerted a negative effect on platinum. In the early 1990s, car manufacturers developed autocatalysts that relied more heavily on palladium as a platinum substitute. This tipped scales in favor of palladium prices and caused spread relationships to dramatically narrow. In 1991, palladium made a low of $78 per ounce. By 1995 the price touched $160 for a climb just exceeding 100 percent. In comparison, by 1995 platinum moved only $40 above 1991 lows for less than an 11 percent change.

Palladium has exhibited approximate four-year cycles, as evident in Figure 5–15. Although platinum and palladium are correlated, the relationship is not exact. We find that both metals have been mined in similar quantities. From 1992 forward, the pace of palladium extraction picked up over platinum whereby there was approximately 20 percent more palladium mined by 1996. Figure 5–16 demonstrates that these metals can diverge into opposite price trends. Notice how palladium moved from lows in February of 1983 to highs toward the end of that year. At the same time, platinum reached highs in June and declined at year-end. This is an important observation because fundamentals are likely to create such situations in the future. Prior to palladium's enhanced role in catalytic converters, we had an assumed 5-to-1 price parity. This decreased to 4-to-1 within the 1990s. Projected usage for both metals suggests this ratio could come in to 3-to-1. Thereafter, platinum's superior efficiency in autocatalysts should hold the ratio steady.

As previously mentioned, a speculative frenzy could be induced by silver and gold. This would change ratios in favor of platinum because palladium has lacked speculative interest. However, it is interesting to note that palladium actually exceeded all metals in its spectacular appreciation during the run-up of 1979–80. Analysts attributed this to the fact that palladium had "farther to go." This logic is faulty because it assumes price level, alone, can determine the velocity and distance of a move. This would challenge the most established principles of the Random Walk Theory. As of this writing, no statistical evidence of price level "dependence" has been published.

Perhaps palladium's most significant price event took place in the spring of 1989 when two professors from the University of Utah announced they had produced a nuclear fusion reaction at room temperature using a palladium cathode wrapped with platinum

F I G U R E   5–15

Palladium Prices 1982–95 Near Contract Basis

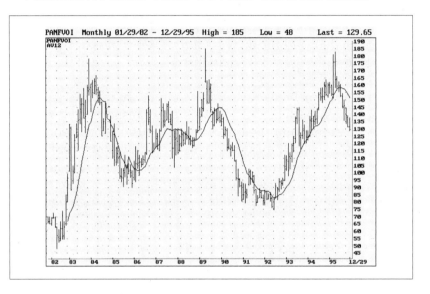

F I G U R E   5–16

Palladium Prices (above) versus Platinum (below) 1983–85 (Note how prices were negatively correlated.)

wire in a heavy water solution. The process was appropriately labeled "cold fusion." The announcement quickly propelled palladium to record highs of more than $180 per ounce in the cash market. As quickly as palladium rallied, it crashed in response to allegations that cold fusion was, at best, a mistake and, at worst, scientific fraud. Figure 5–17 demonstrates the speed of the market reaction.

The unusual breakout witnessed in February 1989 gave rise to suspicions that cold fusion was a sophisticated attempt at market manipulation. It appeared obvious that someone was accumulating palladium just prior to the highly controversial cold fusion press conference. However, investigations revealed that the suspicious price rise was linked to Japanese accumulations related to autocatalysts. If Professors Pons and Fleischmann had

F I G U R E 5–17

The cold fusion announcement sent prices soaring in March 1989. Thereafter, prices quickly retraced as the process was denounced by the scientific community.

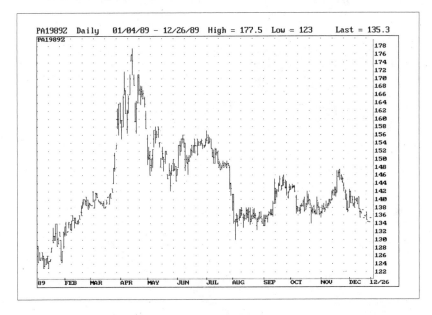

PA1989Z Daily   01/04/89 – 12/26/89 High = 177.5 Low = 123   Last = 135.3

been speculating in palladium prior to their announcement, it was never proven.

Cold fusion prospects did have a structural impact on pricing. From 1989 forward, there was a steady rise in the amount of palladium allocated for fusion experimentation. In addition, cold fusion perked speculative interest in accumulating the metal—just in case. By 1990, estimates for cold fusion experimentation ranged from 5,000 ounces to as much as 50,000 ounces. In 1992, the range expanded to between 50,000 and 250,000 ounces. These numbers are significant when one considers that they can represent 1 percent to 5 percent of total annual production. Thus, even if cold fusion were a hopeless illusion, the pursuit could still generate enough demand to influence prices.

Palladium is a "thin" market, making speculation difficult. Further, it is not easy to buy the physical metal. A small amount is struck into investment bars by Johnson & Matthey. Some Russian "Ballerina" coins are available through dealers, and some specific "cold fusion" medallions were minted shortly after the 1989 announcement. Essentially, investors are left with the futures markets or deliveries in quantities with 100-ounce increments.

Seasonally, palladium has an erratic pattern with first-quarter rallies in 1979, 1980, 1983, 1986, 1987, 1993, and 1994. The more consistent pattern is a lower drift through the last quarter, which is observed in 1980, 1981, 1984, 1985, 1986, 1987, 1990, 1995, and 1996. As with other metals, price trends tend to span three to five months. This supports a strategy using long-term filters like an advanced thirty-day moving average. There is a basic misconception that once metals break out into a major trend, it is impossible to catch the action. This is merely a psychological aversion to buying in a rising market or selling in a falling market. Certainly in palladium's case, smooth transitions occur from rising to falling prices. Although there are spikes, the extent of these extremes was not sufficient to retrace most pre-existing trend movements. Unfortunately, precious metals traders profile as an impatient crowd. Mainstream investors do not seem to adhere to a longer-term buy-and-hold or sell-and-hold policy regardless of its proven historical efficacy. Figure 5–18 illustrates palladium's price patterns over eighteen years from 1979 through November 1996.

F I G U R E 5–18

Palladium Price Patterns 1979–96

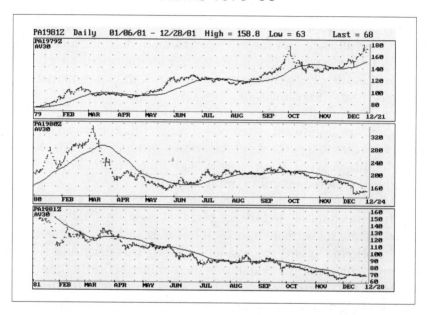

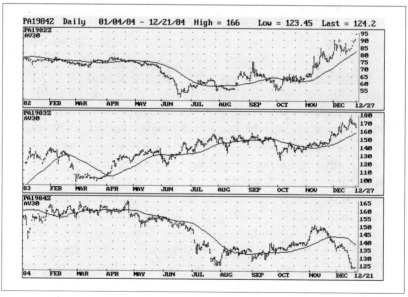

F I G U R E 5-18

Continued

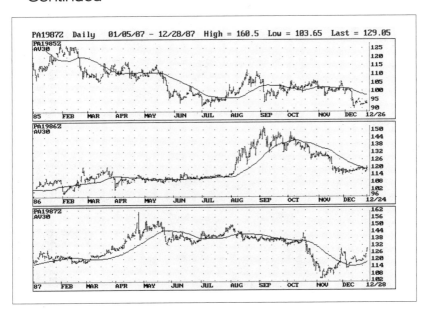

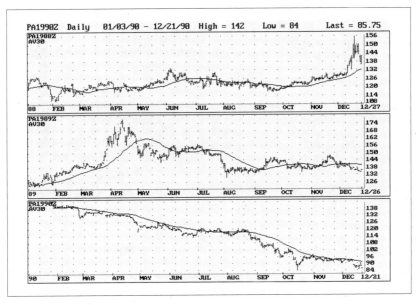

F I G U R E   5–18

Concluded

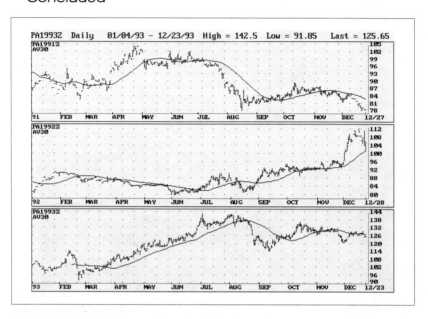

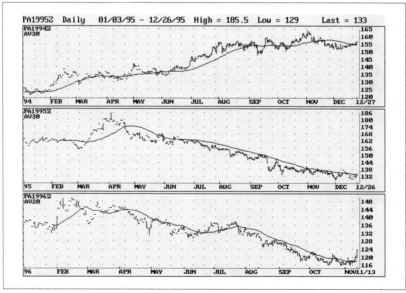

Palladium's propensity to move substantial distances in each of the years from 1979 forward suggests this metal is a better candidate for speculative trading than the more stable gold. Understand that this observation is based on price volatility without any consideration for fundamental factors that can alter gold's inherent picture. History, alone, cannot warn us of pending change.

When Chapter 8 examines the platinum group in greater fundamental detail, you will see that its roles as a catalyst remained critical from the mid-1970s forward. In a debate on the CNBC television network, I engaged a representative of The Platinum Guild regarding the possible elimination of autocatalysts shortly after the transition into the twenty-first century. My research indicated that progress in controlled engine ignition represented the single most significant threat to platinum group price stability. Just as digital photography will decrease silver demand, so must digitally controlled fuel and ignition systems impact prices and demand for platinum and palladium. Yet such developments will not detract from "tradability." You should simply be aware of vulnerability when considering those wonderful platinum coins so frequently advertised in national newspapers and magazines.

CONCLUSION: TREAT METALS AS THE COMMODITIES THEY HAVE BECOME

I have spent countless hours consulting with individuals and corporations about pricing prospects for gold, silver, platinum, and palladium. Too often, reality is obscured by false perception. How often can we claim we have actually examined price history? I believe the basic chart illustrations in this chapter debunk several widely held illusions about stability, volatility, seasonality, and cyclical patterns. With the right perspectives in mind, we can see that precious metals do act like "commodities." They are highly tradable and lend themselves to modern price analysis and speculative strategies. Much of the literature covering precious metals fails to divorce itself from monetary roles and linkages. This failure is so prevalent among mainstream thinking that it distorts reality.

In the 1996 U.S. presidential election, some debate centered around Republican vice presidential candidate Jack Kemp's affinity for a return to a gold standard. Whenever there is a conversation about precious metals, it is almost inevitable that former monetary applications become a topic. In the broadest sense, such references may be appropriate. Successful investors deal in the present rather than the past. The time to deal with metals as monetary instruments is when (and if) nations return to hard asset valuation. Without that development, investors should view metals as commodities.

CHAPTER 6

Gold Fundamentals

Gold is a particularly unique precious metal. Aside from its beauty, weight, and rarity, gold embodies exclusive characteristics including being a noble metal with unparalleled ductility and malleability. It is commonly known that a single ounce of gold can be extruded into a viable wire exceeding five statutory miles in length. Alternatively, an ounce of gold can be flattened into a sheet covering more than 100 square feet. My earlier allusion to gold as a "constant" goes beyond its monetary association. Gold is virtually indestructible. It never tarnishes, is highly resistant to any form of corrosion, and is totally recyclable. These properties are the backbone of gold's industrial value. Although there are no absolute statistics covering gold production and consumption throughout the ages, industry groups estimate that as much as 90 percent of all gold ever mined still exists as tangible supplies today.

USES OF GOLD

Gold has excellent reflective properties and selective transparency as a thin coating. This makes it useful for optical coatings and spectrum-specific mirrors. There are rumors that the world's most

T A B L E 6–1

1996 Gold Consumption by Major Category
in Metric Tons

Jewelry	2,749
Bar Hoarding	300
Electronics	209
Other	110
Dentistry	66
Coins	92
Medallions	35
Total	3,561

powerful "sunbeam" weapon is designed around a highly polished gold concave mirror. Gold is used to coat window glass and space visors. The list of special properties continues with gold's remarkable heat and electrical conductivity. Gold is highly coveted as contact material in electrical and electronic switches. Even with the enormous move into fiber optics, telephone companies rely on gold as the critical element in sensitive switching mechanisms.

Still, with all of gold's exceptional characteristics, the greatest demand comes from fabricated jewelry and hoarding. Table 6–1 and Figure 6–1 provide a snapshot of gold usage as of 1996. Figures are based on estimates derived from Gold Fields Mineral Services, Ltd., the United States Bureau of Mines, and the Gold Institute.

Jewelry

As global wealth increases, we can expect a dramatic rise in gold jewelry fabrication. Of all potential growth areas, jewelry holds the most promise in the absence of any monetary crisis. From the beginning of time, gold body ornamentation has been a preoccupation of humanity. As mentioned in the opening of this text, gold has particular symbolic and religious significance in many cultures. After World War II, the distribution of wealth was divided into three categories: Western Industrial, Eastern Bloc, and Third World. However, for the purpose of understanding gold demand,

1996 Gold Uses (in tons)

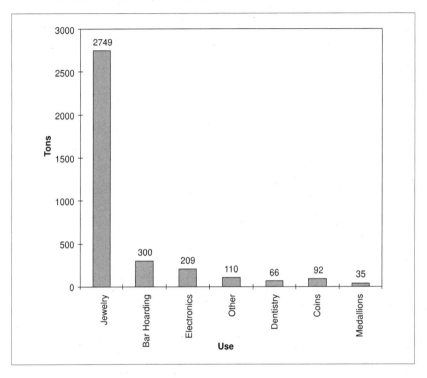

a more refined perspective is helpful. This is because cultural impacts on gold are likely to be extremely important as the entire world moves toward more uniform wealth distribution.

As an example, we know that Chinese customs place a heavy emphasis on gold as a symbol of marriage. To be sure, China's gold jewelry fabrication moved from approximately 19 tons in 1986 to more than 190 tons in 1996. This 900 percent increase can be compared with U.S. usage, which grew from 116 tons in 1986 to 150 by 1996—only a 29 percent increase. The rate of growth in China and nations with similar customs is indicative of an important pattern. Table 6–2 and accompanying Figure 6–2 show the rate of increase in China's fabrication for the ten years from 1986 through 1995.

T A B L E   6–2

Chinese Gold Fabrication of Jewelry (in tons)

1986	19
1987	21
1988	24
1989	26
1990	35
1991	125
1992	190
1992	173
1994	203
1995	191

F I G U R E   6–2

Chinese Gold Jewelry Fabrication, 1986–95

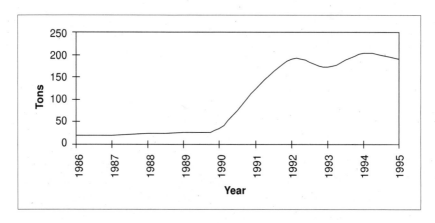

Since the liberalization of investment restrictions in China from 1990 forward, gold has experienced a dramatic rise in fabrication demand. However, these statistics may not reflect an accurate consumption picture because fabrication can be targeted for export. This is particularly true for Italy, which stood as the number one fabricator as of 1996. Italy is the world's largest manufacturer of gold chain for export. Unfortunately, internal consumption statistics are estimates based on observed exports and reported gross consumption. Using this basis, China's internal usage moved from 125 tons in 1989 to 297 tons in 1994. This 138 percent increase supports the fact that gold demand is expanding in China at an increasing rate.

China is joined by India as the second largest potential gold consumer. Here, gold is religiously significant as well as a custom. As of 1996, India was estimated as the largest consumer, with internal usage approximating 326 tons and total fabrication at 400 tons. Within the enormous population, gold adornment is the custom from the smallest nose pin to the most lavish necklaces and bangles. As with China, India's consumption will increase in proportion with expanding wealth. From 88 tons in 1986 to 304 tons in 1995, India experienced a 245 percent increase in fabrication demand during ten years. This fuels the argument that gold is on a collision course with surging prices. Although production experienced equally impressive expansion between 1986 and 1995, slopes of various consumption lines took a lead over gross global output.

Any forecast based on these facts requires extreme caution. In 1985, several reports called attention to the same circumstances. Based on information available at that time, many investors concluded that prices would leap higher within that year because industry sources claimed production had reached a peak. In fact, production was just beginning to accelerate. Any contention that gold production could not be expanded was clearly as wrong then as it would be now.

Nine recognized regions comprise the global gold market, as follows:

1. Europe
2. North America
3. Latin America
4. Middle East
5. Indian Subcontinent
6. Far East
7. Africa
8. Australia
9. Former Communist countries (Russia, China)

T A B L E 6–3

World Gold Jewelry Fabrication (in tons)

1986	1,277
1987	1,325
1988	1,638
1989	2,029
1990	2,181
1991	1,992
1992	2,340
1993	2,739
1994	2,541
1995	2,604

F I G U R E 6–3

Global Gold Jewelry Fabrication, 1986–95

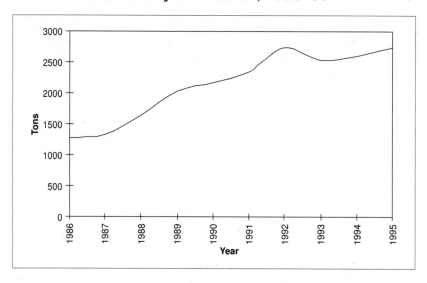

Total world consumption derived from these regions moved from 938 tons in 1986 to 2244 by 1995 for a 139 percent increase. Consider the overall growth as represented in Table 6–3 and Figure 6–3.

The nine regions can be divided into two markets: mature and developing. North America is an example of a mature region with modest expansion compared with developing China, India, and the Far East. In the background are sleeping giants like the Commonwealth of Independent States and Latin America. Based on emerging industrial markets, it is fair to assume monetary stability will come, allowing citizens to accumulate wealth at an increasing rate. The key to any long-term evaluation relies on the speed and consistency of the actual accumulation rate relative to any decrease in demand among mature markets. Although detailed data for each country within each region is available, such analysis mainly serves as an exercise rather than a conclusive study. If anything is known about jewelry demand, it is that patterns change quickly. For our perspectives, it is sufficient to attempt an assessment of more general patterns. Figure 6–4 plots fabrication for the major regions from 1986 through 1995. Here, it becomes obvious that demand is being led by developing regions. The series is correlated with Table 6–4.

Gold enthusiasts quickly point out that demand patterns suggest explosive upward price movements when considered alone. Obviously, supply must enter the price equation. Yet there are extremely strong arguments for a pending shortage if jewelry sector demand follows slopes in Figures 6–3 and 6–4. Demographic studies support prospects for continuing demand. However, wealth and purchasing power depend on price. As previous chapters explained, pricing from 1986 through 1995 was static to lower while purchasing power was just breaking out in developing markets. When demand offsets supply enough to increase prices, elasticity enters the equation.

Politically, one of the most significant developments impacting gold and many other markets is the Internet and communications evolution. When there is a free flow of information, governments find it difficult to control markets. At best, two-tiered systems controlled by governments fall victim to black markets. At worst, governments fall victim to revolution. As the global market emerges and matures, most gold barriers are likely to dissolve. Gold can be quoted, bought, and sold electronically.

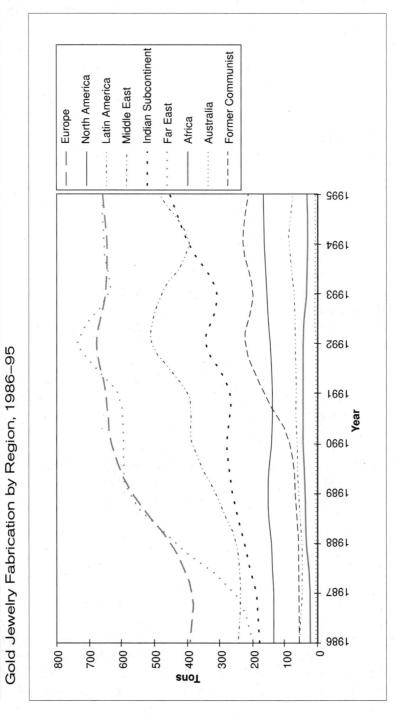

F I G U R E   6-4

Gold Jewelry Fabrication by Region, 1986–95

TABLE 6-4

Gold Jewelry Demand Patterns by Region, 1986–95

Year	Europe	North America	Latin America	Middle East	Indian Subcontinent	Far East	Africa	Australia	Former Communist
1986	392	133	56	244	176	198	21	4	53
1987	383	134	46	237	190	253	22	4	55
1988	450	142	47	249	223	432	32	4	59
1989	565	153	59	310	259	574	35	5	70
1990	629	142	60	382	278	592	43	5	82
1991	647	136	66	398	269	614	43	4	163
1992	678	146	70	505	339	733	44	4	220
1993	649	156	73	477	306	642	33	6	199
1994	644	164	88	396	394	655	29	7	227
1995	659	166	77	484	454	660	31	6	212

Deposits can be held in any location and electronically transferred in an instant. How can governments regulate ownership in the Information Age?

Two-tiered markets like those maintained in India become virtual impossibilities. This means that exponential growth markets like India, China, and the Far East will be driving forces on the demand side of the price equation. The Commonwealth of Independent States (CIS) and Latin America must also be considered to be powerful forces as societies mature and accumulate wealth. Although the slope of the CIS curve stalled into 1991, with time this huge producer will consume more of its production. An upper class and middle class are forming. The population diversity suggests that an elite "white Russian" class cannot grow sufficiently to absorb substantial amounts of gold jewelry. I believe this theory is misplaced because it is based on the former Soviet Union. The large Moslem population has gained status with the formation of the CIS. Their affinity for the yellow metal is strong and supports an argument for a reversal in buying patterns well into the twenty-first century.

Bar Hoarding, Coins, Medallions

Physical gold investing encompasses bars, coins, and medallions. Together, they make up the second largest demand category. However, physical investing represents a double-edged sword because hoarding can lead to dishoarding. Indeed, this is a confusing area because it must be analyzed on a net basis. The gold industry recognizes that bars fuel supply as well as demand. Coins and medallions have not been viewed as a source of supply even though they are freely exchanged and the rate of exchange can impact prices. Evaluating investment accumulation is made more complex because figures are difficult to derive.

Two statistics provided a basis for "reasonable" estimates. First, there is new annual gold bar fabrication. This indicates the amount of "new supply." Of course, these bars can become jewelry, dental material, coins, medallions, or electronic contacts. There is also an attempt to identify bars placed into investment holdings through storage and transfer statistics. Some accuse the industry of double counting; others claim significant transactions remain clandestine. What is certain is that investment demand is the most critical for generating dynamic price movements. This is the emotional arena that is inevitably responsible for shifting the supply/demand equation.

Unlike jewelry fabrication, which can be viewed as true "consumption," hoarding lacks definitive long-term patterns. Today's accumulation can easily become tomorrow's distribution. Therefore, analysis of this critical area is, in most respects, moot. However, it is worth considering some basic fundamentals. The majority of private gold is held in Western Europe, the Far East, Middle East, India, and China. The United States entered the private investment scene late because U.S. citizens were not able to legally own investment bars until 1975. Surveys reveal that U.S. gold investors opted for coins over bullion. This is because the United States developed few mechanisms or vehicles that facilitated bar ownership.

Patterns of hoarding and dishoarding continue to vary. Factors that seem to affect the process include political change, monetary stability, alternative investments, and wealth. As an example, Saudi Arabia experienced relatively low accumulations from 1985 through 1988, averaging about 4 tons per year. As tensions arose over Iraq's invasion of Kuwait, accumulation leaped to more than 20 tons in the latter half of 1989. During the next three years from 1990 into 1992, the amount averaged more than 25 tons per year. Then, demand plunged below pre-1989 levels with less than 2.5 tons in 1993 and a modest 5.6 tons in 1994. The same uncertainty over the Gulf War was reflected in the accumulations of other Middle East countries.

Japan's accumulation habits are even more pronounced. Although not linked to conflict, gold investment is hypersensitive to economic developments. Japanese investors view gold as a symbol of stability and status. Because Japan is a small island nation, real estate is scarce and at an extreme premium. Precious metals and other hard assets act as supplements to land ownership. Thus, Japan has been the largest accumulator of private gold and platinum hoards. Figure 6–5 shows estimated Japanese accumulations from 1986 through 1995.

F I G U R E 6-5

Japanese Bar Hoarding

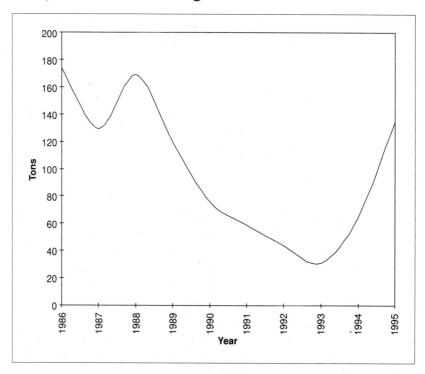

It is apparent that there is no consistent pattern. When amounts are compared against average gold prices during the same period, we see this hoarding has no significant correlation with price. I believe most of the Far East shares a bond with gold. Even without a definitive trend or pattern, I am comfortable with the assumption gold accumulation will continue. Unlike Western nations, which have held the majority of bars as central bank assets, Japan is accumulating private accounts. Political and economic sensitivities that can drive private gold into the market are very different from motivations for central banks. As with jewelry, expect a steady increase in demand from this sector in the Far East.

F I G U R E   6–6

World Gold Coinage

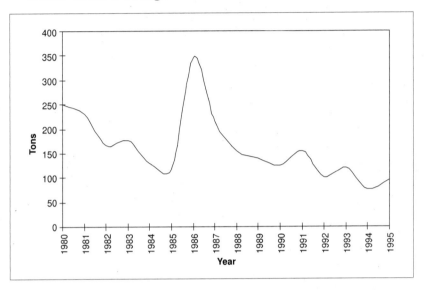

Total world gold bar hoarding has ranged from a low of approximately 200 tons in 1992 to a high of 570 tons in 1989 during the ten-year period from 1986 through 1995. My research suggests that the accumulation pattern will have secular growth approximating 1.8 percent to 2.7 percent per year. Of course, this assumes no monetary crisis to divert investors toward gold on a more permanent basis.

Official gold coinage maintained stability from 1980 through 1986 and steadily declined from 1986 through 1995 reflecting a lack of small investor interest. Figure 6–6 reflects the pattern.

In contrast to official coinage, medals, and medallions enjoyed a steady rise in demand over the same period. Although not enough to offset the decline in government mintage, the private production of gold medallions could be significant. The question is whether this production is stimulated by low prices and curtailed with high prices. My work indicates that elasticity is an important factor. Total world fabrication of medallions increased more than 200 percent from 1986 to 1995. However, this was a move from approximately 10 tons to more than 30 tons. Some analysts claim "bootlegged" Malaysian and Chinese gold counts for more than five times this amount and is not reflected in any official statistics.

The fact is that when gold is affordable, people buy. As prices increase, investment takes precedence over casual accumulation. Casual accumulation could easily conflict with investment demand because higher prices may switch interest from one to the other. I point this out because my earlier discussions about the booming 1979–80 market covered increasing investor participation with increasing prices. In that particular instance, all forms of gold appeared attractive and it is difficult to identify casual accumulation. It is the later data that suggests a reluctance to buy when prices are too high.

Among the growth areas are medallions like the Turkish "Zynet," which celebrates the Islamic circumcision ceremony. According to the Gold Fields Mineral Services, Ltd. *1996 Report,* production of these medallions increased 160 percent from 1995 through 1996 to 13.6 tons. A middle-class family might receive 50 grams, whereas a wealthy son could get two or three kilograms. This is similar to gold exchanged at Chinese weddings or in India. Not all Islamic sects commemorate circumcision with gold. Yet, the world's Islamic population is large and rapidly growing. It is fair to assume that this tradition as well as customs in other countries can sustain reasonable medallion sector growth. However, the statistics on which this assumption is based are recent and within the context of growing global wealth. Figure 6–7 illustrates that medallion fabrication was actually recovering in the later 1990s after a decline from 1980.

Such major emphasis is now placed on demand from the Pacific Rim, China, India, Turkey, and central Asia that it is worth touching on global perspectives. While not necessarily politicized, wealthy nations are "concerned" about issues like global warming and the environment. The altruistic nature of these concerns may, in some respects, represent a smoke screen for blocking industrial progress in the Third World. Understand that many scientific projections call for serious environmental deterioration

F I G U R E   6–7

World Medallion Fabrication

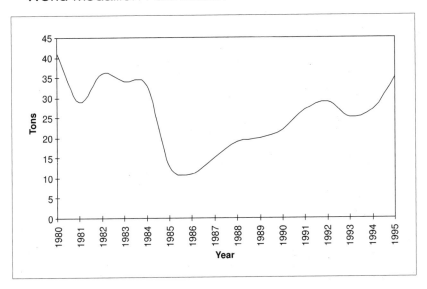

and economic stress if the world, as a whole, adopts living stand-ards similar to those of North America and Western Europe. The "Green" movement may be a "Me" movement because saving the Brazilian rain forest benefits the world more than the owner. It is fine for the United States to decry Brazil's development as long as the United States' standard of living remains unchecked.

I bring this up because any book about markets and global conditions is bound to be off target if conditions change. A book about gold during the 1920s would assume a gold standard. As of this writing, the strong divergence between wealthy and devel-oping nations remains. Within a few decades, the global economic complexion could be completely different. You must keep an open mind when approaching any market. One of the most significant problems facing investors is change. If anything is likely to cause conflict over the next few centuries, it will be resource scarcity. Simply put, there is not enough of anything to support a world living standard as lavish as those of the United States, Japan, and Western Europe. Who will dictate which countries can have and which cannot? This will be important as you look for accumulation trends in precious metals markets.

Dentistry

Once again, wealth is the primary determinant in trends associated with dental use. Two additional developments helped increase dental gold demand since the late 1980s. First, Europe and North America responded to the supposition that silver/mercury amalgam poses a health hazard. It is possible that mercury used to bind amalgam can slowly leach out. This process might accelerate if gold and silver are present in the same mouth.

My review of the dental profession suggests that growth in this sector will meet increasing resistance as alternative reconstruction materials become available. By 1990, dentists were using composite materials with trade names like "Dicore" and "Concept" consisting of glass, ceramics, and resins. These materials are designed to match natural teeth in all respects; color, strength, and temperature reactivity. Prior to 1990, most of these materials were used only cosmetically for front teeth. Increasing sophistication of restoration materials supported use in molars and have shown effectiveness exceeding fifteen years. This trend toward alternative materials will continue and gold fillings may be virtually eliminated by the mid-twenty-first century.

Dental gold consumption increased from 52 tons in 1986 to approximately 62 tons in 1995. Figure 6–8 plots the trend from 1980 forward.

Progress made in developing nations is likely to be offset by technology. Therefore, I do not expect to see dentistry pushing gold prices. If anything, investors could see a dip in this sector, which would probably be insignificant when compared with the more active accumulation areas.

Electronics

Massive growth in sales of computers and semiconductors has been the basis for expanding gold consumption in the electronics sector. Secondarily, telephone and telecommunications switches

F I G U R E 6-8

Gold Dental Use 1990-95

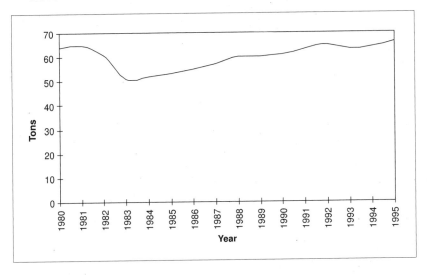

have added to demand. As global modernization continues, the consumption trend continues upward. As explosive as electronics and telecommunications industries have been, gold consumption has been somewhat less spectacular. Better plating and bonding techniques have reduced the amount of gold used for contacts and bonded components. This is a price-sensitive area. Alternatives like nickel/silver alloy and palladium have made inroads. Circuits previously incorporating gold are now configured with less expensive materials. In addition, circuit boards are smaller with more functions on single chips and "chip sets." The result has been a stabilization of gold consumption from 1980 through 1995.

Based on trends in mobile communications and growth in developing nations, I feel confident electronic consumption will double before 2015. This sector experienced modest growth from approximately 195 tons in 1986 to 210 tons by 1995. Digital cameras as well as experiments in gold-based superconductors lead me to believe investors will experience steady 2 percent to 3 percent annual growth beyond the year 2000. There is also a high probability the space industry will increase consumption with new projects in the global push toward space stations and planetary exploration.

Gold's ductility and resistance to oxidation make it essential for critical applications. This is why companies like Toyota boast about using gold in the air bag circuitry of their Lexus automobiles. Of course, the amount used for air bag contacts is extremely small. The more important applications are in switching mechanisms and plug contacts.

Other Applications

The gold industry breaks out other applications with a primary emphasis on plating. Gold is used to enhance reflective properties of window glass, is a reflective coating for hardware used in corrosive environments, and can be used for medical implants and in medicines. In reality, the scientific community is just waking up to applications for gold that could have profound long-term effects on demand and pricing.

Although much of the work with gold in new technologies is proprietary, the most significant potential applications have received some public recognition. Electroactive polymers hold the promise of new lightweight batteries. Experiments with gold and gold salts suggest that this venerable metal could unlock room-temperature superconductivity. Gold, itself, is not the best conductor. Copper and silver have less electrical resistance. However, the stability of gold and its interaction under various controlled conditions imply a host of undiscovered applications as of this writing.

The cost-to-benefit ratio may stand in the way of widespread gold consumption in new areas like superconductors or gold plasma lasers. Certainly, superconductive wires would require huge quantities that would, in all likelihood, price gold out of the market. Still, it is worth keeping an eye out for new uses. The use of gold plating and decorative material doubled in the ten years from 1986 through 1995. From approximately 64 tons in 1986, the estimated consumption rose to nearly 120 tons into 1996. There was an unusual increase in gold leaf used for signs and building decorations beginning in 1994. Some analysts attribute this rise to restoration of historical sites in China and other Far East countries. As long as the price remains under approximately $450 per ounce, gold can be effectively used as industrial decorative material. Gold leaf can be as thin as 1/100th of an inch.

DEMAND IN GENERAL

All sectors combined give clear signals of increased gold consumption through the 1980s and 1990s. Economic patterns point to rising demand possibly accelerating within the first decade of the new millennium. Jewelry will lead the growth curve and investment will represent the balancing wheel. The assumption of steady and controlled demand growth depends on the demonetized gold status. Demand can instantly change if governments return to this metal as monetary backing; this is a threat that will not fully dissipate until central banks truly abandon reserves. Thus, we live with a significant wildcard.

As previously discussed, the wildcard has too many implications for any intellectual exercise. Will our gold be taken away? Will new generations ever embrace this metal as money? The supply side holds some answers to these questions, but not a solution you can invest on!

SUPPLY

Gold supplies fall into two categories: newly mined and aboveground inventories. The nature of these categories is somewhat unusual because it relates to gold's unique personality as an "investment" or store of value. We may analyze other markets in a similar fashion when we refer to existing home sales and new home sales. Other precious and base metals have aboveground supplies like scrap and stored inventories. By far, stored gold represents the most striking two-level supply situation. Thus, central bank demand must be measured against central bank sales. Private bar hoards are a source of supply as well as demand. In the macro sense, aboveground supplies depend on newly mined gold. This is why some analysts view existing gold as less important than new production. Yet, we know the impact disinvestment can have on prices. Because investing or speculating is the underlying theme of this text, the enormous global gold stash cannot be ignored.

The trend in gold production is solidly up. Beginning with the price boom of the late 1980s, gold discoveries and mining technology have combined to increase gold production 1,000 percent. From 1980 through 1990, the United States increased gold production from 30 tons to 294 tons. In other words, U.S. output was 880 percent more in 1990 than in 1980. From 1990 through 1995, production moved from 294 tons to 330 tons. Although this was only a 12 percent increase in the following five years, we should keep in mind that the 36-ton increase is more than 100 percent of the entire U.S. 1980 output. This is similar to arguments about stock market corrections in reverse. The 500-point crash of October 1987 would be small in 1996 terms since the market index more than doubled. Western production moved from 960 tons in 1980 to 1755 tons by 1990; an 83 percent increase. Over the next five years, output increased by 135 tons, or 7.7 percent.

The massive acceleration in production during the 1980s is attributed to advances in extraction technology and increasing by-product production. First, "heap leaching" enabled companies to economically remove gold from low-grade ores and surface soils. This development alone elevated South Carolina from a virtual nonproducing state to the ninth largest gold-producing state by 1992. As new technology was applied to existing properties, output grew at unexpected rates. In fact, increasing production defied all previous studies and expectations as evidenced by findings of the Gold Commission under the Nixon Administration. One of the essential flaws in gold as a monetary backing was inadequate supply and insufficient capacity to expand supplies in the future. At one point, there were estimates that gold production must double to satisfy monetary requirements—an impossibility based on assumptions during the Nixon years. Would we have held to a gold standard if we knew of potential new supplies?

As of the late 1980s, industry literature suggested that production technology had reached some practical limits. Therefore, much of the new production would depend on new discoveries. Historical precedents and continuing technological developments proved this assumption incorrect. First, by 1993, mining companies barely scratched the surface of cutting edge mining and extraction innovations. The emphasis during the 1980s was primarily enhancing efficiencies of known oxidation/reduction methods. Global production remained a mix of high-tech chemical processing and low-tech manual crushing with mercury removal. On the horizon were *Thiobacillus ferrooxidans*, bacteria that actually eat low-grade ores, leaving behind more easily processed gold-containing counterparts.

In 1996, approximately 35 percent of global gold production was attributed to "refractory deposits." Without becoming too technical, gold is bound in pyritic deposits containing hazardous materials like arsenic and arsenopyrite. Conventional extraction methods call for expensive "roasting" processes that present environmental problems and challenges. Still, substantial progress in heap leaching of oxidized gold ore as well as autoclaving continued to increase yields from low-grade ores at decreasing costs. The new "bugs" actually digest the unwanted materials away from the gold. The added advantage to using bugs is the lack of hazardous by-products. The arsenic remaining after digestion is inert. The process does not use highly poisonous cyanide leaching. More remarkably, bacterial oxidation is efficient and provides reductions in both capital and operating costs. In 1994, Newmont Mining received a patent for its specialized version of bio-oxidation.

There are several varieties of ores, and each requires a specific processing approach. During the 1980s, surface mining gained momentum because capital costs and risks associated with deep shaft mining favored this alternative. Moving to the next millennium, robotic mining and computer modeling are likely to return the industry to deep hard rock mining. One of the largest expenses associated with shaft mines is environmental control. The deeper the mine, the hotter the temperatures. When miners work in a mine, air conditioning alone can add huge expenses. Water containment presents further problems. However, sophisticated remote control and computer analysis reduce requirements for human intervention at rock removal and transport stages. Equally important, monitoring equipment detects stability of hard rock formations in

anticipation of "rockbursting." This is an explosive event resulting from stressing structures adjacent to ore removal sites.

Research and development add up to more gold at lower
relative extraction costs. This is why the growth curve is likely to rise
in the future. Based on known commercial technology, I anticipate
a renewed upward steepening of the supply trend line. The slowdown in growth toward the end of the 1980s and through the 1990s
should reverse and be sustained at that level for at least several
decades. This does not take into consideration more esoteric and less
commercial processes that may emerge to make gold an abundant
commodity. By far the largest known resource is seawater. Tremendous quantities of gold are held captive in our oceans, and removal
has been overly expensive. Two new technologies were being tested
for commercial feasibility when this book was prepared for press.
Electroactive polymers were being developed to remove gold from
both ores and seawater. In addition, electroactive/reactive filtration
systems showed promise for low-cost extraction of gold and other
metals. If the systems are practical on a commercial scale, some
estimates for extracting gold from seawater are as low as $50 per
ounce. This would be an amazing evolution in the gold market and
could easily return us all to a gold monetary standard. Is the world
ready for plentiful gold? Based on demographic implications, vast
amounts of gold could not appear at a better time!

By the mid-1990s the top twenty gold-producing countries
ranked as shown in Table 6–5.

Figure 6–9 depicts the graphical ranking.

Geological surveys indicate that production will accelerate
in the United States, Canada, and Indonesia, and South Africa's
output will level off or decline into the twenty-first century.
Experience tells us that surveys are not always reliable into the
future because technology can alter perspectives. Reports indicate
the type of deposits found in South Africa will become less
economically attractive; hence a projected decline in South African output. This means it is possible that the United States will
assume the number one rank if Russia does not capitalize on its
vast resources. However, we cannot discount the impact of
growth in general. Figure 6–10 illustrates the growth pattern from
1980 through projections for 1996 by major region.

T A B L E 6–5

Gold Production by Country Rank

Rank	Country	Approximate Output (tons)
1	South Africa	550
2	United States	330
3	Australia	255
4	Canada	155
5	Russia	145
6	China	140
7	Indonesia	75
8	Brazil	70
9	Uzbekistan	65
10	Papua New Guinea	55
11	Ghana	53
12	Peru	52
13	Chile	50
14	Philippines	30
15	Zimbabwe	27
16	Colombia	25
17	Mexico	21
18	Venezuela	17
19	Bolivia	16
20	North Korea	15

What is immediately noticeable is the production acceleration beginning in 1984. Both technology and the aftermath of surging 1979–80 prices played roles in formulating this trend. The steeper slope carried through until 1990. Thereafter, the most significant technological innovations were discounted and growth moved into a steady state.

Perhaps the most fascinating contradiction associated with supply analysis and projection is the surge in new discoveries despite falling prices from 1985 forward. From Greenland to South Carolina, gold was coming out of "them there hills." By 1995, Indonesia burst onto the scene. New properties are developed with the latest technologies. My research shows impressive

136

F I G U R E 6-9

Top Twenty Gold-Producing Nations

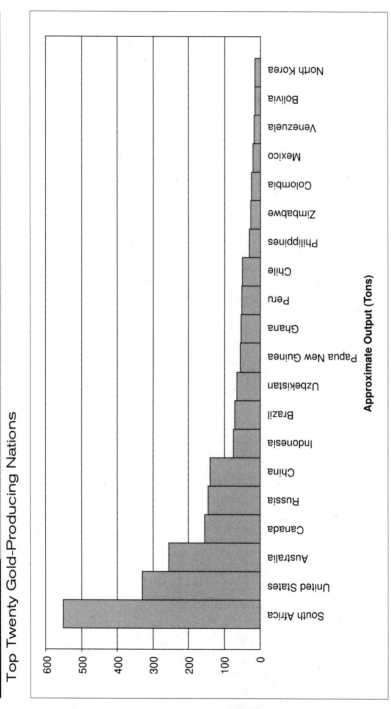

F I G U R E   6–10

Gold Production by Region

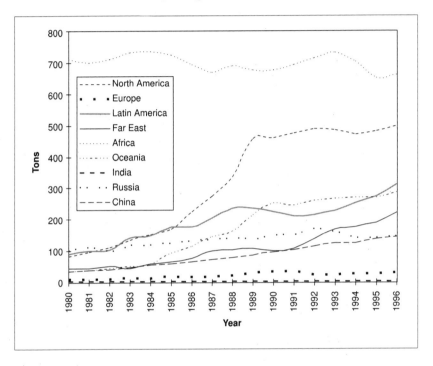

potential along the copper-rich western ridge of South America encompassing Chile and Peru. This region will increase contributions through the first half of the next millennium. Pacific Rim resources were barely touched as this text was being penned.

Total mine production demonstrates a relatively smooth upward trend. Based on regression analysis extrapolation, mining companies may double new production each decade. Statistics cannot necessarily measure resources in the ground or future economic viability for production expansion. Therefore, assumptions based on straight line or even curvilinear projections require caution. Two decades of experience provide a sound foundation for expecting gold mining to increase along the path illustrated by Figure 6–11 in the least.

F I G U R E 6–11

Total New Gold Production

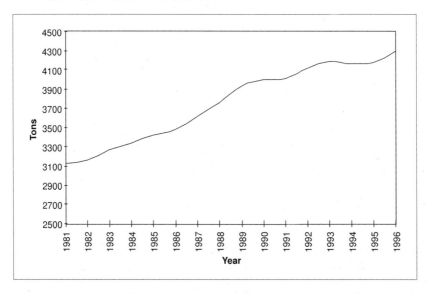

Finally, I previously touched on official gold reserves as adding to potential supplies. Global politics associated with economic systems suggest gold might be abandoned as central bank reserve assets. Indeed, the trend through 1996 was toward divestment. Table 6–6 illustrates this pattern among industrialized nations from 1985 through 1994.

Despite the discussions about a move away from central bank gold reserves, the ten-year trend reflected in Table 6–6 does not indicate a mass exodus from this metal. However, toward the year 2000, central bank gold sales were accelerating. In particular, the European Community (EC, now the European Union) began adjusting reserves to balance currency parities in its unification attempt. From a global perspective, Figure 6–12 demonstrates the easing of reserves.

Figure 6–13 provides a snapshot of approximate ownership as of 1995. The tallest bars represent totals for industrial central banks and the world.

T A B L E 6-6

Central Bank Reserves in Millions of Ounces

Year	Belgium	Canada	France	Germany	Italy	Japan	Nether-lands	Switzer-land	United Kingdom	United States	Total Industrial Countries	Develop-ing Oil	Develop-ing Nonoil	IMF[2]	Bank for Int'l Settle-ments	World Total
1985	34.2	20.1	81.9	95.2	66.7	24.2	43.9	83.3	19	262.7	896.5	43.8	98.5	103.4	6.7	1,149.00
1986	34.2	19.7	81.9	95.2	66.7	24.2	43.9	83.3	19	262	895.6	43.7	100.3	103.4	6.4	1,147.70
1987	33.6	18.5	81.9	95.2	66.7	24.2	43.9	83.3	19	262.4	894.3	43.6	99.1	103.4	6.1	1,144.90
1988	33.7	17.1	81.9	95.2	66.7	24.2	43.9	83.3	19	261.9	895.1	42	103.3	103.4	6.6	1,150.50
1989	30.2	16.1	81.9	95.2	66.7	24.2	43.9	83.3	19	261.9	891.5	42.1	101.3	103.4	6.6	1,144.40
1990	30.2	14.8	81.9	95.2	66.7	24.2	43.9	83.3	18.9	261.9	889.4	41.5	101.6	103.4	7.8	1,144.20
1991	30.2	13	81.9	95.2	66.7	24.2	43.9	83.3	18.9	261.9	887.3	42	102.2	103.4	6.6	1,141.50
1992	25	9.9	81.9	95.2	66.7	24.2	43.9	83.3	18.6	261.8	877.4	42	101.7	103.4	6.8	1,131.30
1993	25	6.1	81.9	95.2	66.7	24.2	35.1	83.3	18.5	261.8	860.4	42	100.1	103.4	8.6	1,114.60
1994[1]	25	4	81.9	95.2	66.7	24.2	34.8	83.3	18.4	261.8	867.3	42	99.7	103.4	7.3	1,109.60

[1] Through October only.
[2] International Monetary Fund.
Source: American Metal Market.

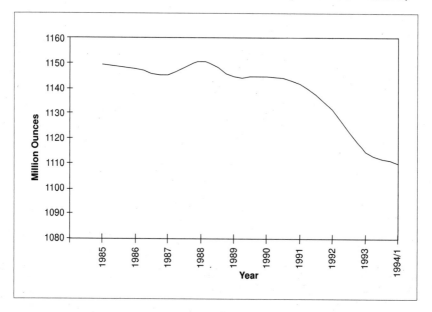

F I G U R E 6–12

World Central Bank Gold Reserves (1994 estimated)

The potential to flood the market with gold is likely to exist for a long time. However, even with increasing liquidations toward the end of the 1990s, gold was able to sustain a reasonable price level through central bank sales.

Central banks will never dump gold reserves. If any liquidation process is to take place, sales will be clandestine during long periods. It would be self-defeating to cause a decline in the value of reserve assets through improperly executed sales. Assuming world economic systems permanently abandon gold, the size of reserves and pattern of sales through 1995 suggest these assets will be depleted within a twenty-five year span. This places a zero date around 2020.

The impact on prices cannot be determined because economists cannot project economic conditions forward that many years. In fact, experts have difficulty forecasting more than a few

Central Bank Gold Ownership by Country

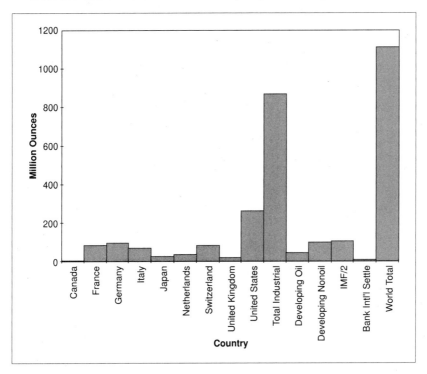

months with any certainty. A steady liquidation would mean a stable economic environment. The conclusion is that gold will lose value or parity if reserves are added into the flow of new production. Experts do know that total reserves are finite. At some stage, sales can exhaust these stored supplies if no future accumulation policy develops.

THE BIG PICTURE

The prevailing trend points to increasing gold supplies that appear able to keep pace with demand. In the absence of monetary or political crisis, gold will remain a "commodity" balanced between supply and demand. As the premier monetary metal, gold has been displaced by monetary technology that includes rapid information transfer and processing as well as synthetic valuation vehicles like futures, options, and derivatives. Nations can always move back to asset-backed currency. However, this is not likely with the present pace of global economic expansion.

Religious and cultural attachments to gold are likely to be diluted by modernization. Old traditions give way to new thinking more quickly in our Information Age. Will Chinese families accumulate gold as they become more wealthy, or will they prefer televisions and personal computers? In short, gold, as a symbol, is being challenged.

The fundamental appeal of gold will never be completely expunged. There will be a practical value to this precious metal. However, technology suggests the scales are tipped toward more economical production and lower selling prices. Even if there were a monetary disaster, gold would return over time to its status as a rare commodity.

Silver Fundamentals

$\mathbf{S}$ilver's qualifications as a major industrial metal as well as a monetary standard provide a more diversified foundation for demand than some industrial metals offer. Regardless of inflation, silver's applications extend to photography and imaging, electronics, welding, mirrors, medicines, water treatment, jewelry, tableware, batteries, glass coating, and medallions. The three fastest-growing applications involve electronics, batteries, and water treatment systems. The largest single use is associated with photographic imaging. Silver has unique characteristics including conductivity, reflectivity, and photosensitivity. Until recently, there were no viable alternatives to silver for various applications relying on its unique properties. However, during the 1990s, technological innovations began to impinge on silver's territorial imperative.

SIGNS OF DECLINE IN THE DEMAND FOR SILVER

Just when there was an industrial resurgence in silver-based mirrors, science began delivering monomolecular "dielectric mirrors" that represent the most highly reflective surfaces known.

These special mirrors are spectrum-sensitive and can reflect almost 100 percent of the specified light. Although the use of dielectric mirrors for large-scale reflective surfaces was still experimental as of 1997, there is little doubt these scientific marvels have the potential to cut back silver consumption in the industrial mirror sector.

Equally threatening is the development sterilization processes using ultrasonics, ultraviolet light, and X-rays. By the mid-1990s, several companies were introducing "irradiated" foods with a theoretically indefinite shelflife. This same process was making progress in water purification systems. Because new applications have been based on the antibacterial properties of silver, alternative bacteriostats are important considerations. In India, two water purification systems have been considered for residential use in small villages. One is a silver filtration system; the other uses ultraviolet light. The major advantage of using silver is its independence from an external energy source. However, this edge could be lost as energy distribution systems rapidly emerge in undeveloped countries.

The booming electronics industry holds the greatest potential for silver demand. Here, too, the white metal races against technological innovation. Small silver oxide batteries used for watches, cameras, hearing aids/medical devices, and other applications represent a huge growth area. Unfortunately for silver, electroplastics have been discovered that may produce equally potent lightweight batteries. Further, these plastic devices appear to be rechargeable and environmentally friendly. Thus, on all fronts, silver's industrial infrastructure appears challenged.

From a production standpoint, silver has gone through an almost total transformation. Prior to the 1960s, silver production was dominated by dedicated mines. Today's major supplies come as by-product from other mining operations. Therefore, silver output is highly dependent on demand for base metals like copper, nickel, zinc, lead, and tin. In addition, silver is produced as a by-product of gold and platinum. This means silver is directly linked to macroeconomics affecting base metal markets. Surging demand for housing, automobiles, and durables could skyrocket base metal demand and values while severely depressing silver, gold, platinum, and palladium. The implied inflation of roaring economies may actually develop an inverse relationship to silver prices if industrial applications for this metal decline.

Effectively, it's a whole new world requiring entirely new perspectives to become successful as an investor in precious metals. Under old rules, silver operated in accordance with normal supply/demand/price correlations. High prices stimulated more production from primary sources. Low prices encouraged cutbacks in mining operations. When silver was unable to sustain lofty levels following explosive 1979–80 price trends, market dynamics completely changed. Much of the dedicated silver production became uneconomical. Yet, by-product output was unaffected. Understand that when silver is produced as a by-product, supply fundamentals are no longer independent. Therefore, the silver price will not necessarily impact production.

Certainly, if silver advanced above $20 per ounce, there would be a question of whether the by-product was driving the primary market or vice-versa. At some price level, silver production could assume a primary role. However, this scenario seems unlikely when investors evaluate technological and economic developments. First, stimulating fundamental demand would require some new and substantial applications. The price elasticity of these applications would need to support a high price. As of 1996, the most extensive use of silver came from two categories: photographic and electrical. Together, these applications accounted for more than 70 percent of U.S. usage. World consumption follows approximately the same proportions as in the United States. Therefore, it is fair to assume that silver's future heavily depends on progress in these areas. Figure 7–1 provides a graphical view of consumption; Table 7–1 lists consumption patterns within each category since 1977.

From 1977 forward, total U.S. silver consumption has been declining to flat. This pattern reflects both domestic usage and a proportion of exports. The two largest conventional photographic filmmakers remained Kodak of the United States and Fuji of Japan. Because film is sold across a global market, consumption

U.S. Silver Consumption by Type

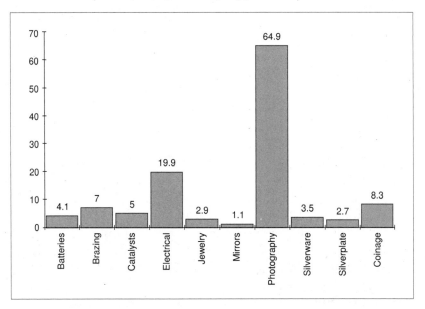

figures by country can be distorted because we don't identify final usage. Figure 7–2 plots the total consumption trend, whereas Figure 7–3 gives a snapshot of the two major categories.

As the charts reveal, both curves remained relatively flat from 1991 forward. The key to any forecast is based on the impact of new technology. Here, the electrical future for silver is bright because computer and communications industries are growing. As previously emphasized, the photographic horizon looks dismal. The worldwide estimate for consumption pegs photographic usage at approximately 33 percent. My studies indicate this figure may be understated, as referenced in Figure 7–4.

As of 1996, approximately 44 percent of new production was consumed by photographic processes that included consumer and industrial photography, medical and industrial X-rays, lithographic printing, and other film-based imaging. With just under half of all new production dedicated to this area, we can assume photographic applications are critical in the price equation. It

T A B L E 7-1

Silver Consumption Patterns by Category

Year	Batteries	Solders	Catalysts	Electrical	Jewelry	Mirrors	Photo-graphic	Sterling-ware	Silver-plate	Total Industry	Coinage	Total
b	5.8	12.4	8.9	31.3	8.1	2.1	53.7	16.7	6.8	153.6	0.1	153.7
1978	6	11	8.2	30.8	6.8	1.9	64.3	17.9	7.3	160.2	0	160.2
1979	4.6	10.9	5.6	33.5	5.4	1.9	66	13.1	8.1	157.3	0.2	157.4
1980	6	8.5	3	27.8	5.9	0.7	49.8	9.1	4.4	124.7	0.1	124.8
1981	3.8	7.7	3.8	26.4	5.4	0.6	51	4.4	3.9	116.7	0.2	116.8
1982	4.2	7.4	2.4	27.7	6.3	1	51.8	6.6	3.3	118.8	1.8	120.7
1983	2.6	5.8	2.4	26.3	6.9	1	51.8	7	3.2	116.3	2.1	118.4
1984	2.7	5.9	2.4	25.6	5.8	1	55.3	3.6	3.5	114.8	2.7	117.5
1985	2.5	5.6	2.4	27.5	5.8	1	57.9	3.5	3.7	118.6	0.4	118.9
1986	3.7	6.4	2.3	27.4	4.6	1	55.4	3.9	3.7	118.9	10.3	129.2
1987	2.4	5.6	2.4	22.7	4.2	1	60.2	3.8	2.5	115.3	12.2	127.5
1988	2.5	5.3	2.6	23	2.9	1.1	62.5	3.5	2.6	112	7.9	119.9
1989	2.8	5	2.8	23.5	2.4	1.1	65.2	3.4	2.7	120	6.8	126.8
1990	3	5.2	3	22.8	2	1.2	68	3.5	2.8	125.3	9.1	134.4
1991	3.1	5.7	3.3	18.3	2	1.1	66	3.5	2.8	118.7	9.1	127.8
1992	3.1	6.2	3.8	18.3	3	1.2	64.4	3.9	2.9	118.9	8.1	127
1993	3.3	6.1	4	18.8	3.3	1.3	65	4	3	121.1	8.9	130
1994	3.5	6.6	4.1	19.1	3	1.1	65.5	4.1	2.8	109.8	8.7	118.5
1995	3.7	6.9	4.7	19.7	2.9	1.2	65.7	3.8	2.7	111.3	8.5	119.8
1996	4.1	7	5	19.9	2.9	1.1	64.9	3.5	2.7	111.1	8.3	119.4

F I G U R E   7-2

Total U.S. Silver Consumption from 1977 to 1996

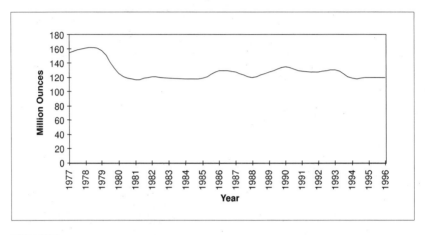

FIGURE 7-3

Silver Photographic and Electrical Uses

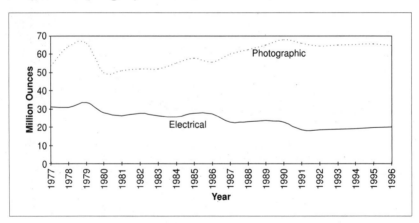

seems truly amazing that little attention was focused on the future of film as of the writing of this text. Although new imaging technologies were virtually exploding on the scene, the potential impact on silver demand was ignored by investors and analysts.

There was once a discussion among audiophiles concerning the future of the compact disc (CD) when it was initially intro-

World Silver Usage (million ounces)

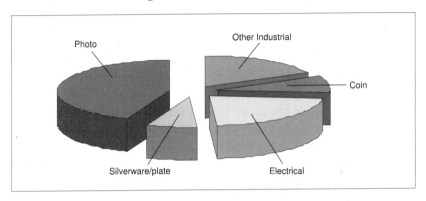

duced. The consensus was that the CD would never gain main-stream acceptance because it was more expensive than vinyl records and the installed base of record players was too extensive for any new technology to gain a foothold. The CD was forecast as an esoteric technology that would be embraced only by the most discriminating ear and enhanced pocketbook. Of course, the CD took over the music market within half a decade. By 1994, it was almost impossible to buy vinyl records in a record store or a turntable at a stereo center! I bring this up because digital and other filmless photography is on the same track.

Consider that the home movie camera became virtually extinct within the single decade of the 1980s. This was the initial indication that silver's largest demand sector was facing trouble. The first cameras were analog. However, the jump to digital recording was rapid. By the early 1990s, digital still-shot cameras with computer interfaces were introduced within comparable price ranges to high-quality 35mm cameras. By 1997, there were more than thirty popular digital cameras with retail prices ranging from $199 to $10,000.

Along the medical front, low-radiation X-ray was introduced for dental and medical applications by companies like Schick Technologies, Inc. with its CDR™ imaging system. Instead of film, units record X-rays onto disk files and display pictures on screen.

If printouts are required, special printers output negatives or positives. No silver or developing is used in these processes. Conventional X-ray film has a high density and high silver saturation. Therefore, the use of digital imaging in this area significantly cuts down on commercial demand.

Finally, the printing industry was moving away from cutting and stripping film negatives to produce lithographic plates. The alternative process converts images from computer files directly into printing plates. Further, electrostatic and ink jet technologies allow high-speed and high-volume full-color printing with no plates. The Silver Institute predicted a slow migration toward nonfilm technologies. This was based on the assumption that printers would not spend the required funds to upgrade. However, print industry sources indicated the pace of conversion and equipment upgrade was accelerating faster than anticipated because "direct imaging" significantly improved quality while cutting costs.

By the late 1990s, Kodak introduced the Advantix® film that combined conventional silver-based technology with a magnetic strip for encoding processing instructions. Inside sources stated that this new film was a stopgap measure to protect huge revenue streams associated with film development. Everything from paper to chemicals represented a massive investment and income source for Kodak, Agfa, Fuji, and others. The installed base of developing machines and one-hour photo stores is truly threatened by the advance of digital imaging.

Although a quality differential seemed to justify using film over digital imaging, arguments favoring filmless technology are overwhelming:

- Environmentally, digital imaging is clean with no developing processes, no chemicals, and no significant expertise required. Conventional photography uses sizable amounts of fresh water and involves toxic materials.
- Digital resolutions as low as 640×720 pixels exceed the maximum line screen used for newspaper and magazine printing. This means that higher film resolution cannot produce a visibly better picture when reproduced by a

printing press. Thus, the quality argument loses most of its validity when considering the capabilities of the human eye and what we can reproduce onto paper.

Certainly, high-resolution computer imaging can exceed conventional film. Spy satellites have the ability to read license plates from miles away in space! The use of more photosensitive receptors and better image compression technology holds the promise of progressively higher-quality computer images. Thus, the future of silver-based photographic processes appears dim as of this writing. With more than 40 percent of the market in question, can other applications take up the slack?

The advance of digital imaging is likely to take a toll on silver values. As prices decline, elasticity will probably boost consumption in other areas. Silver oxide batteries could become more competitive. Brazing usage might rise. However, silverware, silverplate, mirrors, and jewelry are not sufficient growth markets to completely fill the gaps. By the time demand for consumer photography takes hold in populations of China, India, and the Third World, film may already be obsolete. Growth predicted by the silver industry does not seem feasible.

Figure 7–5 illustrates world industrial silver consumption by the major nations, and Table 7–2 lists the data in tabular fashion. It is important to notice how volatile patterns have been within relatively short periods. Consider that production is usually more stable because capacity tends to grow or contract within the capital constraints of the mining industry. Although a strike in Peru or Chile can temporarily impact production, capacity remains intact. However, demand is more fickle. Everything from consumer sensitivity to industrial activity impacts near-term demand.

After a significant decline during the early 1980s, silver advocates began to hang hopes on a recovery that moved almost steadily from 1985 through 1992. Figure 7–6 plots the total industrial consumption for major consuming nations.

There is little doubt that the trend toward the end of the 1900s was toward increasing industrial consumption. If fact, nothing within the statistics indicated a decline in usage relative to earlier

Silver Use by Major Consumer Nations 1973–95

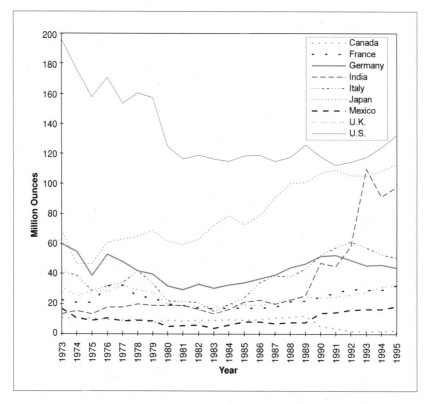

discussions about technological displacement. Although digital imaging was on the scene before the new millennium, it did not seem to have a significant effect on rising demand. Yet this perception is somewhat deceiving. What is missing from the equation and evaluation? First, while demand was rising, the slope of the curve was adversely impacted by alternative technologies. Equally important is the fact that growth was a function of increasing global wealth. The speed of wealth accumulation was greater than the introduction of alternatives to silver. Therefore, the statistics should not be viewed independently from other fundamental developments.

T A B L E 7-2

World Industrial Silver Consumption by Major Nations (in Millions of Ounces)

Year	Canada	France	Germany	India	Italy	Japan	Mexico	United Kingdom	United States	Total
1973	10.4	22.5	60	13	41.5	69	16.5	31	196.4	522.5
1974	10.3	21	55	15	38.6	46.5	10.2	25	176	470
1975	10.3	21	38.9	13	28.9	46.4	8.8	28	157.7	407.7
1976	9.3	31.8	52.9	18	32.1	60.7	10.2	28	170.6	484.7
1977	9.1	32.6	48.1	17.6	33.8	63.2	8.6	32.2	153.6	459.9
1978	9.6	24.6	42	20	41.8	64.9	9.1	29	160.2	452.4
1979	7.3	24.1	39.8	19	33.3	68.8	8.6	27.6	157.3	448.2
1980	8.7	19.8	31.9	19	21.8	61.5	4.9	19.5	124.7	364.3
1981	8.5	18.9	29.3	19	21.5	59.6	5	18.4	116.7	355.4
1982	9	17.1	32.7	16.1	20.8	63.2	5.7	18.1	118.8	361.4
1983	8.9	16.5	30.3	12.9	15	72.1	3.5	17.7	116.3	356.5
1984	9.3	17.1	32.2	16.1	19.4	78.8	5.5	19.2	114.8	376.2
1985	9.1	17	34.1	20.9	23.9	72.6	8	19.1	118.7	500
1986	9.6	17.1	36.3	22.5	33.7	78.5	7.7	19	118.9	541.6
1987	10.4	17.6	39.1	20.1	38.6	90.9	6.9	21.1	115.1	537.5
1988	11	21.3	44	22.4	38	100.4	7.1	22.8	117.5	572.8
1989	12	22.1	46.7	25.6	43.2	100.8	7.2	24.6	126	604.9
1990	4.6	24.5	51.6	46.8	52.4	107.3	13.6	24.1	118.2	668.8
1991	3.8	26.9	52.2	44.9	57.4	109.3	14.3	24.7	112.3	672.3
1992	1.6	29.7	49.3	58.1	61.1	105.4	15.6	26.3	114.5	687.7
1993	1.6	29	45.6	109.9	57.4	105.5	16.4	27.6	117.4	729.4
1994	1.6	29.2	45.8	91.2	52.8	108.5	16.1	31.2	124.3	715.8
1995	2	32.3	44.1	97.5	50.8	112.7	18.5	32.3	132.2	741.6

Source: *Commodity Research Bureau Yearbook*; CRB InfoTech CD-ROM.

F I G U R E   7–6

Total Industrial Silver Consumption by Major Nations

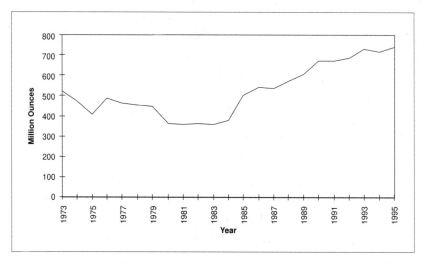

Silver Coinage

Coinage is a category that has been traditionally separate from industrial usage. Aside from the official status of coins as money, supplies are frequently provided from government reserves for collectibles. Like gold, silver has been stored as a reserve asset. Governments have viewed silver reserves as strategic as well as monetary. Figure 7–7 plots coinage by major industrial nations.

Relatively weak demand for official coinage was originally reflected by the move away from monetary linkage. The appearance of renewed demand from the mid-1980s forward is directly correlated with the release of coinage as a profit center. The U.S. silver dollar was minted to sell at a premium over spot prices. The Canadian $5 silver Maple Leaf was produced for the same purpose, as were several other government issues. Toward the end of the 1990s coinage profit margins were thin because of increases in marketing costs relative to demand. The exceptional stock market performance shadowed hard asset performance. The coin market became extremely depressed.

F I G U R E   7-7

Silver Consumption by Nation

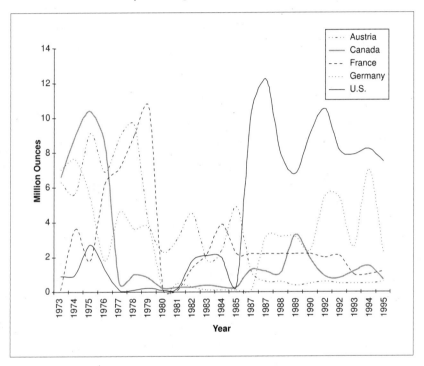

The overall role of silver coinage is small and not likely to be a pivotal factor in price performance. However, earlier discussions in this text suggested that a low silver price could encourage a return to circulated coinage. At some point, silver's market price could fall below practical face values for coinage. For example, a move away from silver-based film might decrease demand to a point where prices fall to $1 per ounce or less. This would make the one-ounce U.S. silver dollar a "true value" coin. Nickels, dimes, and quarters based on appropriate weight ratios would be at market value. An exact $1 per ounce price might be too close for comfort. The U.S. Treasury might not want the risk of seeing silver move above face value because this would encourage hoarding. Solutions would be to debase or have a market price well below $1 per ounce.

Why move back to silver coinage? After all, composite coins work fine. In addition, earlier chapters mentioned the possibility of plastic coins in the future that can be encoded with tracking information. Silver coins offer no advantage other than perceived value. Silver is a known and accepted form of exchange. It can restore or maintain confidence in a nation's money supply. Confidence is the foundation of all monetary systems. Without trust, there is no viable money. Even with no reason to question confidence, it may be advantageous to foreclose any possible loss of faith by instituting silver coinage. Thus, silver could be a preemptive strike against a confidence crisis.

Use in New Technologies

A discussion of silver demand would not be complete without considering prospective technology. Silver's unique photosensitive properties may extend beyond imaging into the digital domain. The very technology that can spell disaster for demand today could become tomorrow's salvation. There are "chemical memory" devices based on silver, including today's smart cards that store data, and even dynamic memory that uses ionic characteristics to represent binary values. Those who are "up on the technology" may be aware of computing systems based on light circuits rather than electronics. "Photonic" computers may become a reality and silver is a major consideration for bridging the gap between light and electricity. The potential growth for computing applications could rival film in two respects. First, silver storage devices may be used to record images. Unlike film, which is recycled, silver computing and storage components are likely to have much longer useful lives. This implies that less scrap will be available.

It seems ironic that silver might return to provide images after being displaced. However, any revolution in silver technology will take time. Do not forget that production may not keep up with demand. With this in mind, let's examine the various sources for the white metal.

SUPPLY

The majority of global mine production comes from eight major producing countries. Based on production figures compiled by the Silver Institute from surveys of top producing mining entities, Mexico was leading silver output, with approximately 75 million troy ounces in 1995. Next in line was Peru, with 61 million; the United States, with 50 million; the CIS, with 45 million; Canada, with 38 million; Chile, with 34 million; Poland, with 32 million; and Australia, with 30 million. It is easy to see why analysts assert that silver supplies are highly susceptible to significant political disruptions. The next two largest producers were China and Bolivia. The political, economic, and labor stability in more than half the major producing nations has been questionable. Strikes and monetary adjustments have been responsible for several impressive price trends. However, the progress toward more democratic government and capitalistic economies was changing supply concerns during the 1990s.

Total mine production has been decisively rising since the mid-1970s. Figure 7–8 plots world mine output by major producers through 1995. Price sensitivity adversely affected silver in the early 1990s when prices turned sharply lower. However, statistics may be skewed because much of the data reflects *shipments* rather than *actual production*. Inventories held by producers could have accounted for moderate production that was marketed when prices became more favorable during 1995 and 1996.

Silver is obtained from the ores argentite, cerarygrite, pyrargyrite, stephanite, and proustite. It is a component in base metal mining that includes lead, tin, copper, and zinc, and in precious metal extractions with gold, platinum, palladium, rhodium, and related elements. Prior to secondary production, silver mines were primarily dedicated to supplying the treasuries and major industrial users. Prices were fixed by ratio against gold, and elasticity was relatively static.

Currently, supply fundamentals are a function of demand for metallic counterparts. As mentioned, increasing demand for copper, lead, tin, and zinc will, by default, increase the amount of

F I G U R E 7–8

Total World Silver Mine Production

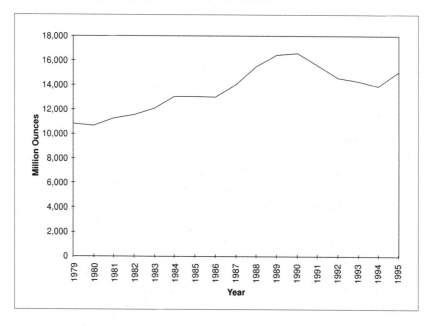

silver. This is an important fundamental consideration because much of the traditional thinking about silver's relationship with inflation remains. Consider that the market has reacted in tandem with rising commodity prices. However, investors were stung several times during the mid-1990s when silver rallies failed to sustain despite bouts of inflation fear. This lack of traditional inflation correlation is directly linked to increasing base metal output. By examining global trends it becomes clear that there is a rapid expansion in industrial metal supply.

Industry projections call for annual increases of approximately 5 percent through 2005 and beyond. Keep in mind that this projection is compounded. Consider that 1995 world production was approximately 14,570 metric tons. The 1999 estimate climbed to almost 17,000. The slope of the production curve suggests shortages will be uncommon.

In general, the growth pattern among significant producing countries displayed in Figure 7–9 supports the trend shown in Figure 7–8. With the exception of the disruption in Kazakhstan, output has been climbing. Because the decline in supplies from the Commonwealth of Independent States was mostly "ecopolitical," silver experts know that several regions, including Kazakhstan, have substantial reserves and capacity. From the numbers, experts know that some output was literally cut in half for lack of funding. However, multinational companies moved into the former Soviet Union as political foundations firmed. As long as there is improvement in the political climate, progress will be made in all forms of mining.

Toward the end of the 1990s, production technology had improved to the point where several mining companies found it economical to reopen primary facilities. As an example, the Coeur and Galena mines in the United States were given new life in 1996 through a joint venture between Coeur d'Alene and Asarco. In 1997, the Green's Creek mine in Alaska was reopened with projected output between 10 and 15 million ounces per year. This trend is likely to continue with estimated extraction costs after capital depreciation between $0.50 and $1.25 per ounce. It is not difficult to grasp the economics if silver can maintain an average selling price between $4.50 and $5.50.

As an adjunct to our analysis, it is appropriate to examine trends in base metals. According to the Bureau of Mines, approximately 66 percent of the world's silver reserves are linked to copper and lead/zinc ores. Based on 1997 production estimates, these reserves amount to 12 billion ounces. Therefore, future silver production could become completely independent of prices. Copper's extreme spread between costs and selling prices created a surge in capacity from 1991 forward. The resulting silver flooded the market and was responsible for depressed prices. Figure 7–10 plots world copper production.

The copper trend certainly implies secondary silver production was building from 1983 forward. With industrialization increasing on a global scale, copper demand should remain strong. There are no viable alternatives to copper as an industrial metal.

F I G U R E   7–9

World Silver Production by Selected Major Producers

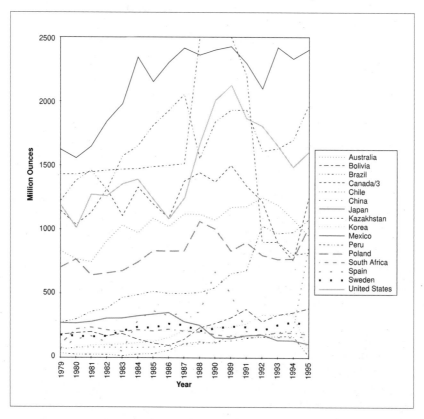

A slight decline in communications use has been seen with the promotion of fiber optics. This is a small component compared with other electronic and electrical applications.

The copper trend is not unique. Consider nickel, as illustrated in Figure 7–11. Toward the end of the 1990s, nickel production was rising after a significant fall in Commonwealth of Independent States' (CIS) capacity. Again, the decline in CIS nickel was due to economic constraints rather than a lack of resources. A recovery in this region was only partially responsible for better

F I G U R E 7–10

World Copper Production 1983–94

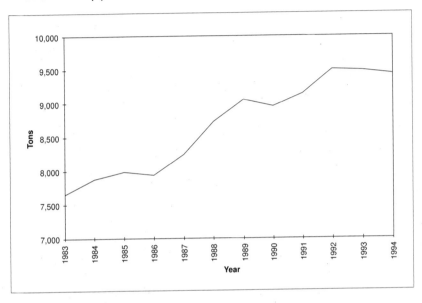

nickel statistics. New discoveries in Central Europe and South America contributed to prospects.

"Efficiency" was the lesson from the energy crisis of the early 1970s. The trend toward becoming "lean and mean" continued with respect to labor, management, and process technology. In particular, heavy industry developed more nimble facilities with greater production flexibility. This carried over into the mining industry, which is notorious for long capital accumulation lead times. Building a new mine is an extremely expensive and time-consuming project. There is extreme sensitivity to price changes because profit margins can become thin or negative between the time a company breaks ground and becomes productive. However, the design of modern mines allows greater output variability with less financial exposure.

The amount of silver held by central banks is no longer significant. The United States has been regularly selling reserves,

F I G U R E 7–11

World Nickel Production 1985–97

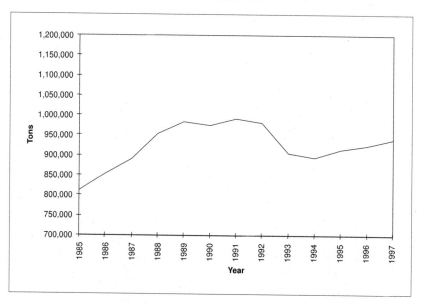

with less than 28 million ounces available in 1996. The market has absorbed central banks' sales without reactions. Unlike gold investors, investors in silver do not focus on government supplies. Of course, a mass dumping would negatively impact prices. But, with less than a year's production stored, this would be a temporary factor.

There has been a great deal of publicity about a pending silver shortage. From 1993 through 1996, statistics suggested that consumption was strongly outpacing supply. My own investigation found this analysis to be flawed. Much of the hype was based on assumed consumption and declines in output, which were events that never materialized. The forecast for massive increases in silver halide film was offset by technological advances in coatings that reduced silver saturation by 10 percent to 15 percent. Silver oxide batteries were challenged by nickel cadmium (nicad).

During the brief time to research this book, new discoveries in Indonesia, the Philippines, Brazil, Australia, Canada, Colombia, Bolivia, Mexico, and the United States actually changed projected production by more than 5 percent.

CONCLUSION

Regardless of the general consensus and the ease with which hucksters can tout silver, I do not see a bright long-term price picture for the white metal. From the perspectives of the late 1990s, silver production will continue to rise as a function of increasing base metal output while demand will encounter serious resistance. New silver-based technologies do not appear sufficient to offset the potential decline in silver halide film. Electronic and electrical demand is small compared with film and there could be substitutes for several promising silver technologies like batteries, water purification, and reflective surfaces.

Once the "poor man's gold," silver has lost much of its long-term investment luster. If prices fall sufficiently, silver may be used for coinage simply to absorb excess quantities. It is sad to conclude that technology will displace this precious metal. Of all the metals explored in this book, silver's outlook appears the most bleak. There are valid arguments for renewed interest and it is wise to keep an eye on technological advances. Silver values will hinge on the furtherance of digital imaging with improved quality and wider acceptance. As with any forecast, time will tell!

CHAPTER 8

Platinum Fundamentals

Platinum is an extremely important industrial metal. Its unique chemical properties make it indispensable for a multitude of processes encompassing everything from automotive industries to fertilizer manufacturing. The primary feature is its ability to promote chemical reactions as a catalyst. Most of us are familiar with automotive "catalytic converters" that reduce hydrocarbon emissions and associated air pollution. However, platinum's use as a catalyst extends far beyond this widely recognized application. As an industrial precious metal, platinum has few substitutes. Although palladium has stepped into platinum's shoes for certain technologies, I believe it is highly unlikely this metal will be displaced within the foreseeable future.

Platinum is an extremely hard metal with a high melting point. It is not reactive by itself and, therefore, extremely stable. Platinum is an excellent electrical conductor, ductile, and relatively malleable. Its usage meshes with other precious metals in jewelry, dentistry, electronics, coinage/medallions, and bar hoarding. Thus, platinum demand has a well-diversified base.

DEMAND

Platinum is a rare metal. This characteristic combines with its versatility to make it one of the most valuable "nonexotic" metals. The adoption of clean air standards around the world helped boost platinum demand through a potentially difficult period from 1993 forward. In addition, explosive growth of computer sales supported platinum's growth curve despite palladium's encroachment on the automotive and truck catalyst market. Demand falls within eight major categories:

- Automotive
- Petroleum refining/processing
- Chemical processing
- Electrical/electronics
- Glass
- Jewelry
- Dentistry/other
- Investment

Figures 8–1a and 8–1b illustrate how platinum demand is divided among its applications.

Over time, usage ratios have been moderately static. However, there was a significant boost in jewelry and automotive use through the 1990s as this metal became increasingly fashionable in the Far East while automotive expansion added to catalyst demand. Toward the end of the 1990s, there was concern that use in catalytic converters might decline based on the potential use of "lean burn" engines. Because approximately 35 percent to 40 percent of annual allocation is for catalytic converters, any decline in this category would have a serious impact on prices.

Automotive Usage

The primary application in the automotive sector is for antipollution devices. These include catalytic converters, oxygen and ozone detectors, and even the tips of hot-burning spark plugs. As world populations mobilize, there will be a steady growth in related

F I G U R E 8–1a

Pie Chart of Platinum Use Categories

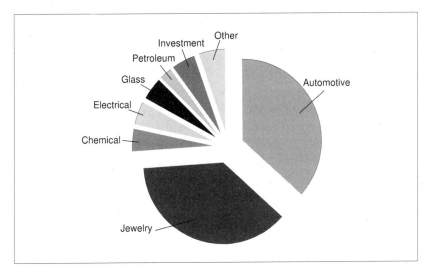

F I G U R E 8–1b

Bar Chart of Platinum Use Categories

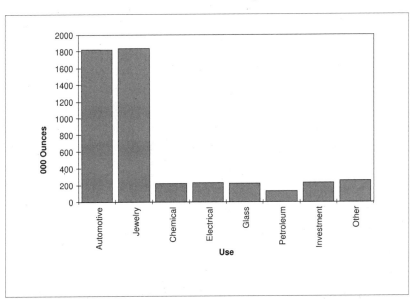

platinum usage including other sectors like petroleum refining and chemical processing. As of this writing, platinum was being combined with palladium and rhodium in a "three-way" converter designed to reduce hydrocarbon, nitrogen dioxide, and other tailpipe emissions. Obviously, increasing demand in the automotive sector will be directly related to increasing car and truck sales.

As is shown in this chapter's discussion of platinum supply, a considerable quantity of platinum can be recovered as scrap because it is not consumed in the converters. Scrap recovery has been an extremely important component of overall supply and will increase in importance as more converters are processed for recycling. Catalytic converters are needed to compensate for inefficient combustion. Depending on weather, tuning, fuel characteristics, and ignition, some gasoline or diesel fuel will remain unburned after each stroke cycle. These unused hydrocarbons are converted to carbon dioxide and water by the catalyst. Incorrect fuel-to-air mixtures are responsible for oxidized gases like nitrogen dioxide. This can be broken into its components of nitrogen and oxygen. Carbon monoxide results from incomplete combustion and represents a deadly gas because it binds with hemoglobin in blood like oxygen, but acts like carbon dioxide. Ozone is also a target of converters.

Because a catalyst may be needed to correct combustion deficiencies, it stands to reason that they could be eliminated if engineers could improve engine efficiency. During the 1980s, transportation companies were experimenting with technology that could significantly increase engine efficiency. These systems use computer chips to precisely mix fuel and air while exactly timing the ignition. Through intricate control of the combustion process, computerized engines accomplish two objectives: higher horsepower and fuel efficiency, and little or no pollution. By 1994, the experimental technology had evolved to include small storage devices that recorded driving conditions like temperature, altitude, humidity, road grade, and driving habits. This information was incorporated into an efficiency algorithm to calculate ideal engine settings. The ultimate objective is to maximize efficiency.

Unfortunately, these advances may have the same impact on platinum demand as digital imaging can have on silver.

There is a platinum lining to the transportation story. Although highly experimental toward the close of the twentieth century, platinum fuel cells provided the possibility of an alternative to petroleum-powered vehicles. The cell converts chemical energy (usually hydrogen and oxygen) directly into electricity, heat, and water. The key to advancing the technology is size and efficiency of the cells. The costs of manufacturing and running fuel cells were too high to be commercially feasible by 2000. Of course, the pace of new technological development tends to accelerate. A practical platinum-based fuel cell could emerge at any moment to have two effects. First, it would substitute for "conventional" power sources. More important to investors, it would render this section of this book obsolete. Approximately 17,000 ounces was dedicated to fuel cell development in 1996—up 7,000 ounces since 1993.

Phosphoric acid fuel cells (PAFCs) and proton exchange membrane fuel cells (PEMFCs) are being designed in Japan, the United States, and Europe at capacities ranging from 50 to 250 kilowatts. Power output is sufficient to power passenger vehicles, buildings, or even small communities. Units have the advantage of being a source of electricity and heat. There are safety and control issues with this technology. Yet these cells appear to be the most likely to absorb quantities of platinum on a commercial scale. It may take several decades before platinum consumption for fuel cells rivals the autocatalyst. Progress in this area leads me to believe there is excellent potential. The time frame associated with the advance of this technology and the potential decline in autocatalysts hints that long-term trends will be subtle and could take half a lifetime to trade from beginning to end!

Figure 8–2 tracks gross autocatalyst platinum demand from 1986 through 1995. Consumption is directly linked to economic conditions that encourage greater or fewer car and truck sales. There is a secular growth inherent in the industrialization movement among Third World and former Eastern Bloc countries that will pick up the pace in overall car manufacturing regardless of

F I G U R E 8–2

Platinum Autocatalyst Use

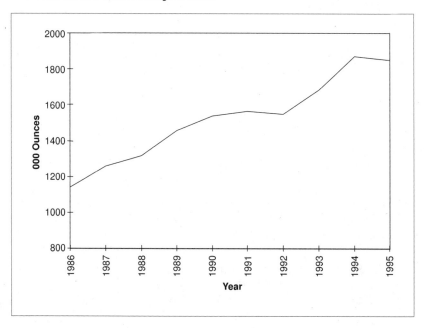

intermittent economic trends. Although investors are bound to see variations in the speed of production, it should be fair to assume demand will continue to increase unless lean-burn technology truly displaces the catalytic converter.

A change in the slope of the autocatalyst consumption curve beginning in 1989 can be attributed in part to the advancement of palladium. As previously mentioned, the growth in palladium use has offset platinum to an extent. Expect this pattern to continue. Yet it is not likely that there will be a total substitution. Palladium is not as efficient as platinum for certain catalytic functions. Most of the palladium-based converters continue using platinum and rhodium. Recall the discussion of spreads between platinum and palladium prices. If the tendency to use more palladium than platinum continues, investors can expect platinum's price premium to deteriorate.

It is essential to keep a watchful eye on technology. Perhaps the most important theme throughout this book is, "times are changing." Even if technology introduction is slow, the speed of market reactions is swift. When Toyota announced its intention to use palladium converters in some exported models, platinum immediately reacted lower while palladium made new life-of-contract highs. Markets are usually anticipatory. Once there is an expectation for technological change, it can be permanently discounted in price relationships. Remember that "relationships" do not always dictate gross price movements. Thus, if there is explosive growth in new vehicle sales, platinum will probably rise. Only the price ratio with palladium, silver, or gold will change.

Jewelry

One of the most significant applications setting platinum apart from other "platinum group" metals is its use in jewelry as a pure or "near pure" element. Platinum's extreme hardness and durability coupled with a rich silver-blue hue make it an extremely attractive metal. Its lack of oxidation has elevated platinum above other "white" metals as the queen. For precious stone settings, platinum maintains an edge over gold because of its strength and its "neutral" color. When the stone is the emphasis, platinum does not detract from the focus with its own color. Yet, platinum's reflective properties can enhance appearance. The traditional price premium compared with gold also adds to its attraction for jewelry. Although there have been moments when gold sold over the platinum price, the consensus is that platinum is (and will remain) the more valuable commodity (see Figure 8–3).

A keen aspect of growth in platinum jewelry is related to skin tone. The most impressive expansion in jewelry demand comes from Japan and other Asian regions. Platinum has more "contrast" against the Asian complexion. This same characteristic began to push demand in India and Africa as well as among ethnic groups in the United States and Canada. Clearly, Japan has displayed the greatest admiration for platinum jewelry. Consider that Japan consumed approximately 1.50 million ounces of platinum as

F I G U R E 8–3

Platinum Jewelry Fabrication

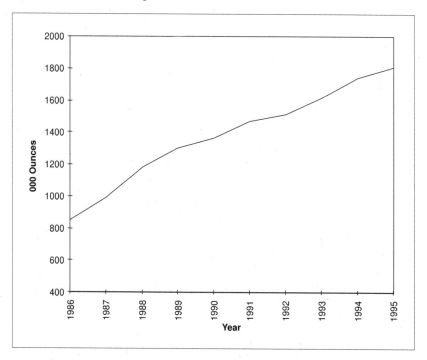

jewelry in 1996 whereas Western Europe accounted for only 123,000 ounces. The North America total came in around 62,000 ounces. Considering that total world jewelry fabrication was approximately 1,840,000 ounces in 1996, Japan accounted for 1.5 million ounces— about 82 percent. This suggests that platinum prices will be highly sensitive to economic conditions in Japan. Any change in Japanese consumption patterns should be carefully observed.

Platinum's durability has made it an increasingly popular material for high-end fashion watches. Platinum watches have been manufactured since the early 1900s. However, its hardness and high melting point made platinum difficult to work. Even in modern facilities, platinum takes a quick toll on tools and dies. After the huge 1980 price surge, there was a tangent desire for platinum timepieces on the wrist. This trend has carried forward.

In the early 1990s, the New York Mercantile Exchange cohosted a remarkable display of platinum watches in New York City. The most expensive platinum and diamond watch fetched a price toward $1 million. The everyday Vacheron Constantin's "Perpetual Skeleton" self-winding chronometer was a meager $73,900! To qualify for a platinum hallmark, a watch can contain only a small amount of alloy (usually copper)—just fifty parts per thousand. From any perspective, platinum watches are not likely to make a potent dent in supplies. The expense alone limits the extent of the market. Investors can take comfort in the knowledge that if there is major growth in this narrow area, the world will be on a fast track to enormous wealth!

Unlike autocatalysts, jewelry displays an almost constant slope. The trend suggests growth stability and modest sensitivity to economic variations. It is true that there is no direct substitute for platinum in jewelry, only alternatives. Because of the high-end nature of platinum settings, bracelets, necklaces, and watches, price elasticity does not appear to be a factor. It is worth noting that jewelry could fill a "demand gap" during the time required for technological innovation/salvation. In Figure 8–4, notice how jewelry accelerated to match the automotive sector.

The steady growth in jewelry consumption and a presumption that global wealth will encourage this trend plays heavily in the price equation. Some experts question the industry's ability for production to keep up with demand. It will be important to see a decline in industrial consumption for platinum to maintain price stability. Of course, there could be a point where the metal's industrial value outweighs fashion. However, if platinum becomes too expensive, demand will ease. Where there is a need, there is usually a solution. Shortages cannot be tolerated when needs are essential.

Chemical Processing

As a catalyst, platinum is important for producing various fundamental chemicals. Most widely recognized are nitric acid and nitrogen compounds, fertilizer components, and synthetic fibers. Chemical usage is fractional compared with autocatalysts and

F I G U R E 8–4

Use of Platinum as an Autocatalyst versus Jewelry

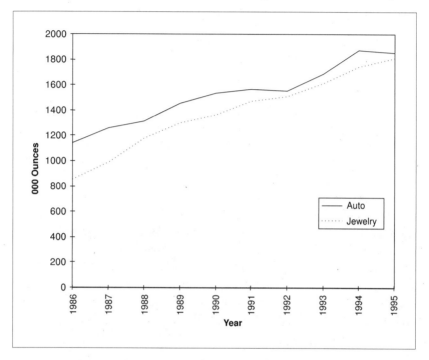

jewelry, as are the other consumption sectors. Yet, platinum's unique characteristics and the lack of an adequate substitute make its use for chemical processing an essential consideration. Specifically, members of the platinum industry are closely observing global agriculture for indications of increasing demand for fertilizer and urea. Increasing global wealth points to greater demand for synthetic fibers. Some materials used to make boat sails require platinum catalysts to synthesize on the front end of the process while platinum dies are used to extrude threads at the back end. The chemical paraxylene is produced using platinum catalysts. This is a feedstock for terephthalic acid, a precursor for several synthetic fibers.

Just when studies showed the possibility of major fertilizer requirements into the first half of the twenty-first century, experiments with petrochemical aerosols appeared to give some plants an ability to absorb nitrogen from the air or increase root absorption. For example, the use of methanol sprays during periods of high-intensity sunlight increased the size and yield of certain melons, corn, wheat, and grapes. The exact mechanism by which plants benefit from this procedure is not clearly understood today. A potential conflict exists between the benefits of petrochemical yield enhancement sprays and environmental protection. A cornerstone of the Clean Air Act in the United States is the reduction of volatile organic compounds (VOCs) from soils, water, and air. Therefore, environmentalists might view methanol spraying with a jaundiced eye. Once again, I call attention to technologies that might have an effect on platinum trends. To be aware is to be prepared.

Figure 8–5 displays the interim trend in demand for chemical usage.

F I G U R E 8-5

Chemical Uses of Platinum

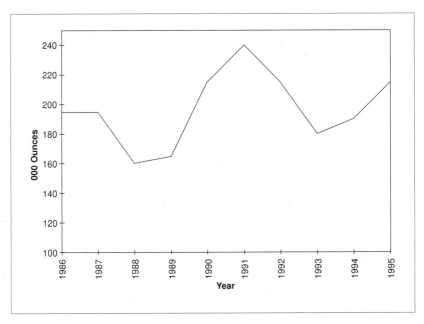

There is an argument for an upward trend in industrial uses based on the short period from 1986 through 1995. The propensity for wide swings reflects linkage to a highly volatile industrial sector. Anyone familiar with chemicals, synthetic fibers, and fertilizer can understand why platinum uses reflect such fluctuations. The observation tells us platinum's chemical applications will be relatively static when compared against other usage. With approximately 4 percent of annual consumption dedicated to chemical processing, the influence on prices should be diminutive.

Electrical/Electronic

Platinum is used for a wide variety of electronic applications. Most of the demand potential comes from computers and related products. Platinum alloys are used to improve magnetic coatings for disks. Super high-density optical storage systems incorporate platinum coatings for read/write surfaces. Microscopic platinum films are used to form platinum silicide wafers that are incorporated in highly sensitive light- and heat-detection devices. These devices are displacing cadmium and mercury because they are less expensive, more reliable, and more accurate.

Platinum is extensively used in thermocoupling devices for measuring temperatures in production processes for glass, metals, and electronic circuits. As process technology expands in size and scope, platinum-based control mechanisms should enjoy steady growth. While minute quantities are used in each device, the number of units can become substantial over the next few decades.

Platinum remains a component of the highly controversial cold fusion process described in earlier chapters. Although palladium is the primary metal touted for this energy-producing anomaly, the experiments announced by Professors Pons and Fleischmann used platinum wire. As an adjunct, platinum demand could surge if cold fusion becomes a commercial reality.

Platinum contacts are critical in particular high-voltage and high-temperature environments. I already mentioned the use in long-life automotive spark plugs. Mission-critical switches also incorporate platinum points. Again, quantities for each unit are tiny, but the number of switches can be enormous. Expect electronic and electrical platinum consumption to increase at a steady pace over time. It is doubtful whether technology will find effective platinum substitutes in electronics/electrical in the near future.

Figure 8–6 gives a perspective on electrical and electronic demand. The powerful increase since 1993 is indicative of a strong personal computer and electronics market. Patterns in the electronic sector point to constant innovation and development. This supports the prospect for growth. Based on the technical slope of

F I G U R E 8–6

Electrical/Electronic Demand for Platinum

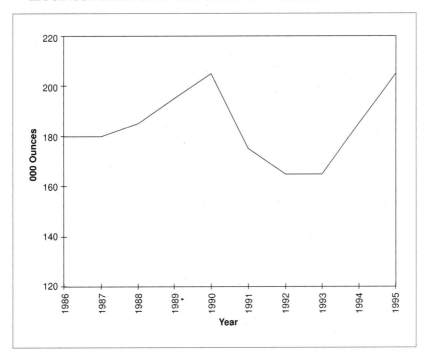

the curve and industry evaluations, investors can expect between 2 percent and 5 percent annual expansion. At such a rate, electronic applications could play a more important pricing role within a short time.

Glass

Platinum is used in dies and process technology for manufacturing high-quality fibers and glass extrusions as well as fiberglass for insulation and reinforced plastics. This sector is sensitive to economic downturns in housing, boating, and consumer/business electronics. The demand for fiberglass insulation moves with trends in housing construction while fiberglass reinforcement is heavily used to make boats, light planes, and even lawn furniture. Figure 8–7 displays demand in this area.

The United States luxury tax was blamed for a severe depression in the boating industry that was reflected by weak fiberglass reinforcement demand. Boats use fiberglass roving in conjunction with epoxy and polyester plastic resins for hull, deck, and interior construction. Obviously, the consolidation in the boat manufacturing business slowed demand for fiberglass and associated platinum use.

The pick-up in platinum demand in the early 1990s was linked to growth in communications fibers, high-resolution cathode ray and liquid crystal displays. Huge demand for portable displays in notebook computers, personal digital assistants (PDAs), cellular phones, beepers, flat panel televisions, digital camera displays, and other devices requiring high-grade glass reversed the downtrend in platinum use in glass manufacturing. Global economic expansion increased demand for conventional fiber insulation, and several automakers have adopted glass-reinforced parts including bumpers, side panels, and even chassis springs.

Although glass accounted for a small portion of annual consumption, it still represents a growth area. Every bit helps when potential investors consider that lean-burn engines could break demand on 33 percent to 40 percent of annual usage.

F I G U R E 8–7

Platinium Consumption in Glass Production 1986–95

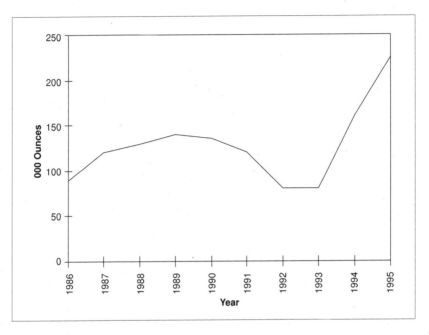

Petroleum and Other Uses

The petroleum industry uses platinum mesh or gauze in cracking processes to refine crude oil and certain feedstocks. Platinum catalysts play a critical role in primary refining and for isomerization octane enhancement. Toward the end of the 1990s, approximately 33 percent of the industrialized nations incorporated platinum/palladium-based isomerization processes compared with less than 15 percent for Third World refineries. The global movement toward environmental protection will push these numbers higher. Based on straight-line analysis, experts anticipate demand reaching between 400,000 and 600,000 ounces as North America and Western Europe move toward full capacity. Thereafter, expect another 100,000 to 300,000 ounces in demand as other regions catch up.

Consumption in this sector can become static because a healthy amount of platinum can be recovered and recycled. Refineries have a rotating inventory of new and used catalytic material. As capacity grows, platinum reserves have a proportional increase. In some respects, the recyclable nature of platinum makes it similar to gold; it's not consumed. There is a certain loss factor associated with reprocessing. However, careful recapturing procedures have made recycling extremely efficient and effective. The petroleum sector could reach "steady state" whereby recycled supplies meet most demand requirements. Under such conditions, only incremental amounts of platinum would be needed to supplement losses or accommodate additional capacity. Figure 8–8 plots platinum use in the petroleum industry.

F I G U R E   8–8

Platinum Use in the Petroleum Sector

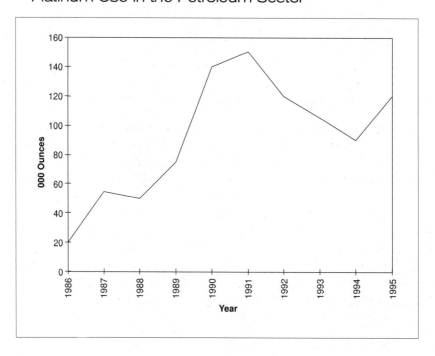

With all of the discussion about clean air and zero emissions, platinum's industrial future appears brighter than that of silver and gold. Although there is a major threat from computerized engine systems, it is unlikely we will eliminate fossil fuels any time soon. Demand in this sector seems assured—for now.

Investment

As with most precious metals, the "swing factor" is investment demand. However, unlike gold and silver, platinum has a far more limited supply with a much greater proportion dedicated to vital commercial processes. This means investor interest can have two motivations:

- The general economic atmosphere can encourage hoarding. This coincides with inflation, confidence, and investor moods.
- There are the potential market "squeeze" situations that arise from labor strikes, mine closings, global politics, and related developments. When traders perceive a squeeze, speculation increases. This makes investment demand difficult to assess over the long term. A squeeze today can easily lead to dumping tomorrow.

The overall pattern moving forward into the third millennium followed a trend away from hard-asset accumulation. Most growth was narrowly concentrated in Japan, which has an appetite for coins, small bars, and large bars. Other world markets are attracted to coins and small bars. For the Japanese, platinum represents a method of hard-asset saving because it is frequently used as a transfer vehicle against the yen. Although parity differentials can be played in currency markets, physical metal provides a measure of safety while value is in transition. In addition, there have been unusual arbitrage situations when the cash market and U.S. futures have been at odds with Japanese pricing relative to the dollar.

Figure 8–9 graphs investment demand from 1986 through 1995. Wide swings are indicative of a speculative vehicle with no

Platinum Investment Demand 1986–95

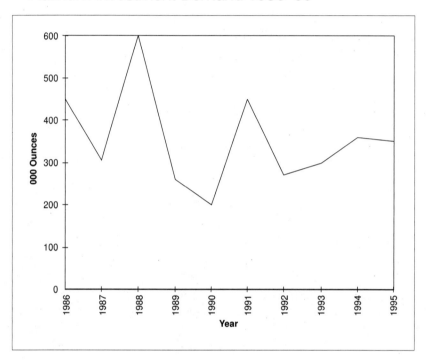

definitive accumulation pattern. As with any hoarding, demand can easily lead to supply as investment changes to divestment. There are no firm numbers for the amount of platinum held as investment hoards. Unlike silver and gold, platinum has not been accumulated by central banks as a reserve asset. The entire hoard should be considered in private hands with the exception of some "strategic" reserves needed for military and related purposes.

It is virtually impossible to predict the behavior of investors from one year to the next. In fact, day-to-day forecasts are almost equally impossible. However, any increase or decrease in investment demand impacts prices and all other applications. If investors move prices too high, industrial processes fall victim to diseconomies. This forces a search for alternatives or relief from the entire application. One of the strongest incentives to perfect

palladium catalytic converters came from the large price difference. Palladium holds an advantage all the way up to a two-to-one
ratio based on 1996 technology and a platinum price of approximately $450 per ounce.

In general, platinum's investment demand follows the precious metals sector. When there is strong demand for hard assets,
platinum is a central element. When paper assets and real estate
offer more potent returns, only die-hard metal advocates find
platinum and its relatives attractive.

Total platinum demand has been growing steadily and will
continue. As global industrialization moves forward, we can expect the slope of platinum's demand curve to steepen. From this
perspective, platinum provides a comfortable fundamental foundation for those wishing to accumulate metal. Yes, lean-burn
engine technology could shake the foundation. It is essential to be
prepared for such a development. Also, the recoverable nature of
platinum could slow demand at some stage. My assessment is that
the world will still need to expand platinum output to accommodate needs through the twenty-first century. This assumes someone does not invent the perpetual motion machine!

Figure 8–10 and Table 8–1 paint the total picture. As the
Platinum Guild frequently points out, this metal is a growing
industry.

The question is whether supply can match the growth curve.

SUPPLY

Most of the world's platinum comes from three major regions:
South Africa, the CIS, and North America. By far the largest
producer toward the beginning of the twenty-first century was
South Africa with approximately 3.41 million ounces. Next in line
was Russia with less than half that amount at 1.34 million. North
America accounted for approximately 250,000 ounces with the
rest of the world at half that amount—just 125,000 ounces. A
graphic representation appears in the pie chart of Figure 8–11.

This makes platinum supply easier to digest, but far more
vulnerable to massive disruption. Most importantly, the two largest sources have been highly susceptible to political and economic

F I G U R E 8–10

Total World Platinum Use

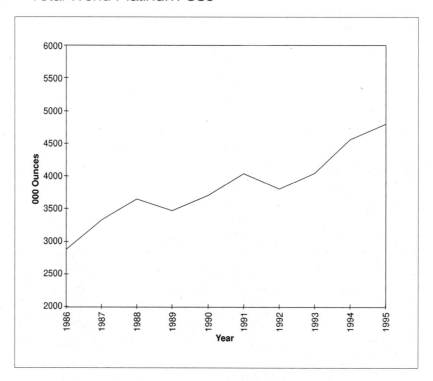

instability. This is the single most significant "excitement factor." At any moment, a strike in South Africa or a mine closing can literally reduce new production to a trickle. Under such circumstances, prices can reach super impressive levels in incredibly short periods.

Both South Africa and the CIS were grappling with new political structures toward the close of the 1990s. South Africa's Black majority rule had not changed ownership of mines, which require huge capital backing to remain operational and expand. Nothing short of absolute cooperation will be required between labor and management into the twenty-first century if mine capacity is to grow. Clearly, platinum is an important income

T A B L E 8-1

Platinum Use by Major Sector

Year	Auto	Jewelry	Chemical	Electrical	Glass	Investment	Petroleum	Other	Total
1986	1,140	850	195	180	90	450	20	130	2,880
1987	1,255	990	195	180	120	305	55	120	3,320
1988	1,315	1,180	160	185	130	600	50	120	3,650
1989	1,455	1,300	165	195	140	260	75	115	3,470
1990	1,535	1,365	215	205	135	200	140	120	3,700
1991	1,565	1,470	240	175	120	450	150	140	4,040
1992	1,550	1,510	215	165	80	270	120	150	3,800
1993	1,685	1,615	180	165	80	300	105	165	4,045
1994	1,870	1,740	190	185	160	360	90	190	4,560
1995	1,850	1,810	215	205	225	350	120	225	4,790

F I G U R E 8-11

Major World Platinum Producers

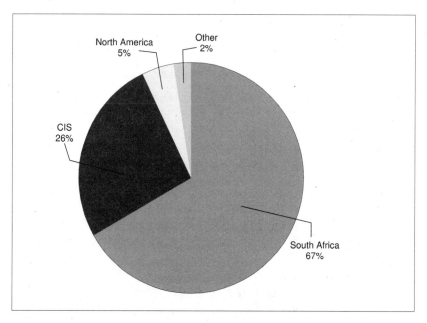

source. The mines provide jobs and revenues along with a measure of economic stability for the government. A small number of entities control most of South Africa's platinum properties. The Anglo American Platinum Corporation operates the Amplats mines inclusive of Rustenburg, PPRust, and Lebowa. In 1996–97, several capital expansion programs were under way to increase output between 10 percent and 15 percent. Steady platinum prices and improved technology were encouraging forces through the 1990s.

Virtually all of South Africa's platinum producers have excellent growth potential. This is based on estimated reserves, new discoveries, improved recovery techniques, and modernization. Weak economics and a lack of increasing platinum values have been an impediment to expansion. Platinum enthusiasts should keep their focus on developments among the South African producers. Aside from following daily news sources, the interim and annual reports from Johnson & Matthey, PLC, give the most concise and reliable assessment of new developments. These reports are not limited to South Africa, but include all the important facts and figures for platinum and her sister metals. Key South African producers include Impala Platinum, Lonrho South Africa, Northam, and Anglovaal Limited. Keep in mind that relationships and corporate structures change. The trend toward multinational mining cooperatives was just under way in the late 1990s. Names, ownership, and entities can easily change.

The CIS was adjusting to possible democracy and capitalism. Platinum represents a solid economic base. Ownership issues within producing states are one facet of the total picture. As of this writing, the CIS was targeted for an international capital infusion free-for-all. Geological surveys indicate the CIS producing regions have the capacity to exceed South Africa to become the number one supplier. In fact, expansion progress was under way from the mid-1980s forward with only a few glitches related to economic uncertainty in the early 1990s and a lack of capital for the Noril'sk Nickel mine, which produces substantial by-product platinum and palladium. Although Noril'sk was literally "the source" for the CIS, my discussions with several informed groups lead me to believe there are extensive and possibly exceptional properties looming for future development. Forward momentum will be a function of price. I would not be surprised to see CIS capacity double within a decade based on vast untapped potential.

The potency of CIS supplies was clearly demonstrated in the spring of 1997. From an equilibrium price of approximately $370 per ounce, disruption in Russian shipments quickly shot prices to almost $430. This 16 percent increase took place in only five weeks. Then, the resumption of Russian sales plunged prices back down in about half the time. Thus, as previously mentioned, supply is likely to play the dominant role in interim trends.

North American production was lifted from a static state with the development of the Stillwater mine in Montana, which was a joint venture between Chevron Resources and Engelhard Minerals. Stillwater is primarily a palladium mine. When falling palladium prices reached a low below $78 per ounce in 1989, the property became marginal. The partner corporations stalled expansion that was critical for developing the full potential earlier. This same price decline was responsible for a slowdown in South Africa and the CIS, too. However, palladium's price revival and strong demand potential have rekindled interest in boosting Stillwater's capacity. Estimates suggest this single property will double production to yield a four-to-one ratio of palladium to platinum.

In Canada, the Ile de Lac region gave birth to Madalline Mines, which subsequently became North American Palladium. This facility was just getting under way as a startup in the late 1980s through the 1990s. After several troubled years, North American Palladium was finally reaching its stride in the mid-1990s. Like the Stillwater Mine in the United States, North American Palladium is primarily a palladium mine (as the name implies). Therefore, financial success depends on strong palladium prices. Original revenue estimates called for profitable operations with palladium as low as $98 per ounce. Based on performance from 1989 forward, there should be a sound basis for expanding palladium mines, which have the advantage of associated platinum production. Canada also enjoys significant nickel resources that produce excellent quantities of platinum group metals in addition to silver and gold. Inco operates the Sudbury mines and was on an expansion program in 1995 that should extend with good base metal price support.

As strange as it may sound, platinum resources have hardly been touched on a global scale. Aside from enormous by-product potential, new geological analysis in Indonesia, China, Australia, and regions north of South Africa including Zimbabwe, Zambia, and Zaire all show potential for developing platinum/palladium mines. Expansion of copper production in Chile and Peru will contribute to increasing platinum supplies.

Figure 8–12 illustrates supply trends from 1983 through 1996. It may not be evident from the graph, however, that advantages held by South Africa and the CIS could be challenged by other producing regions by 2015 to 2020. The number of new

FIGURE 8–12

Platinum Output by Major Region

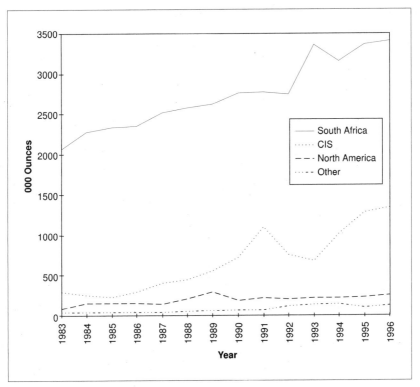

discoveries and the speed within which mines can become operational could increase the pace of world production by more than ten times. This would place "other output" at more than 1.25 million ounces. Surely, South Africa and the CIS will not be standing still. Considering that within the United States, South Carolina went from not producing gold to being the ninth largest producer, anything is possible and probable.

Figure 8–13 shows total platinum production for the same period. Obviously, the trend is up. The question is whether the slope of the production line will begin to increase and when. This becomes a critical issue if we see a pronounced increase in demand.

Total Worldwide Platinum Production 1983–96

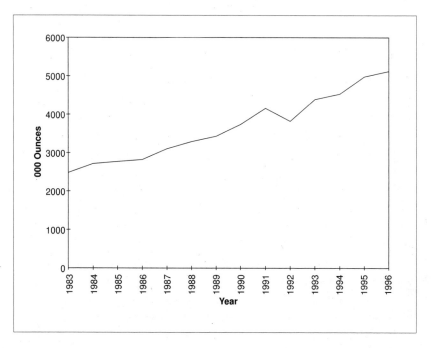

As is demonstrated in Figure 8–14, supply and demand were fairly well matched for the thirteen years spanning 1883 through 1995. The accelerated supply line indicates surplus production and explains why platinum remained static to weak from 1993 forward. It is interesting to note that recovery played a role in maintaining the supply edge. From 1983 to 1995, recovered platinum went from 30,000 ounces to approximately 350,000 ounces, an increase exceeding 1,000 percent. In 1995, recovery matched the entire output of North America and other regions combined. Consider the trend apparent in Figure 8–15.

The slope of recovery is nearly 45 degrees. This exemplifies the fact that platinum is not consumed by its role in catalytic processes. Is it possible the world inventory of recyclable platinum will become sufficient to satisfy demand? The question presents an interesting paradox.

F I G U R E 8–14

F I G U R E 8–14

Platinum Supply versus Demand

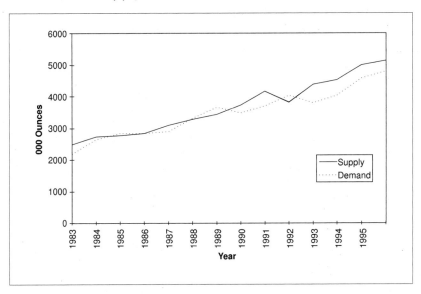

F I G U R E 8–15

Platinum Recovery

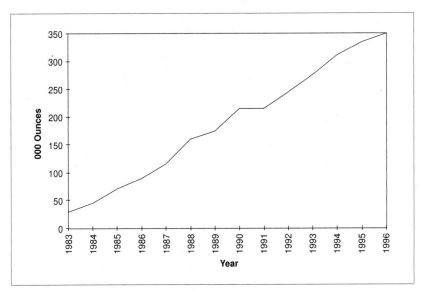

CONCLUSION

Platinum has exceptional speculative potential. The balance between supply and demand is extremely close and delicate. The evolution of more stable economic and political environments within the two major producers (CIS and South Africa) could quell some of the speculative edge. If Latin America is any example, there will be several decades of uncertainty before calm overtakes these two regions. In the meantime, selective fundamental trends should be your focus. Technological challenge to platinum-based catalytic converters is the main demand concern. Recycling is a starting point for tracking supplies. Labor, politics, and economic conditions are all part of the equation. Watch auto sales and remember that the average auto fleet life is approximately seven years. This gives an idea of recycling patterns.

Palladium Fundamentals

Of all precious metals, palladium is the least known. Yet palladium may have the greatest profit potential. As a member of the "platinum group," palladium shares many of platinum's characteristics, including hardness and a high melting point. Even palladium's applications parallel platinum's, including catalytic pollution control, chemical processing, electrical/electronics, and investment. Palladium has a greater use in dental alloying and a far smaller application in jewelry. Palladium's central long-term support comes from its increasing encroachment on platinum along with a favorable price parity. In the late 1980s, new palladium-based catalysts for cars and trucks were developed to reduce platinum requirements while targeting specific tailpipe emissions. This breakthrough established a greater industrial emphasis on palladium and opened the door for more consistent price appreciation.

DEMAND

The proven key to palladium's long-range potential rests with environmental concerns. As more of our world industrializes, palladium will be essential to keep air and water clean. Palladium is used to process industrial hydrogen peroxide that has extensive applications in the paper industry. Traditional paper manufacturing bleaches pulp with toxic chlorine agents similar to products used for household cleaning and laundry.

Environmental regulations seek to reduce chlorine waste. Scandinavian paper mills have implemented highly effective bleaching systems using hydrogen peroxide that decomposes into oxygen and water. Computerized process control provides the same level of bleaching efficiency as chlorine. There is little doubt that hydrogen peroxide (H_2O_2) will find its way into global paper manufacturing. This will place a heavy demand on hydrogen peroxide production and palladium-based process systems.

On a smaller scale, hydrogen peroxide is used for cleaning sensitive electronic machinery and components. Because the electronics sector is expanding rapidly, it is a fair projection that associated demand for palladium will rise.

Palladium is also used in conjunction with platinum to manufacture purified terephthalic acid for the synthetic fiber industry. A number of advances in polyester fabrics and materials should have a positive impact on palladium consumption. Palladium is necessary for industrial as well as consumer fibers. Automotive, housing, aerospace, and boat manufacturing are using an increasing amount of synthetic materials that rely on terephthalic acid. Synthetic fibers are definitely a "growth industry." The 1996 breakdown of palladium's primary uses is illustrated in Figure 9–1.

As of 1996 palladium consumption was concentrated in electronics and electrical applications, followed by autocatalysts and dental uses. Unlike the demand for platinum, palladium demand is less likely to suffer if autocatalysts are replaced with lean-burn technology. The overall demand picture appears solid.

The biggest speculative story affecting palladium began in March 1989 during a press conference at the University of Utah in Salt Lake City. Researchers Stanley B. Pons and Dr. Martin Fleishmann went public with their process for "fusion in a jar." Because their fusion took place at room temperature rather than at millions of degrees, their discovery was called "cold fusion." The cold

Primary Uses of Palladium in 1996

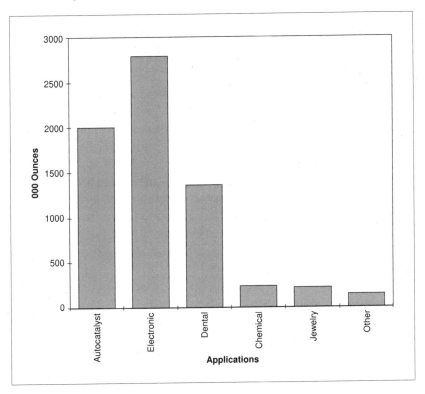

fusion announcement came on the heels of Toyota's announcement of its intention to use palladium in catalytic converters for several car models. Palladium raced to more than $180 per
ounce. Within a matter of weeks, the scientific community condemned cold fusion as "junk science." According to conventional
theory, such a process was impossible. Therefore, palladium
quickly retreated from its lofty levels to lows below $80 per ounce
in 1993.

The cold fusion debate never died; it simply went into hiding.
Each year since the 1989 announcement, scientists from around the
world gather to share experimental data at the annual Cold Fusion

Conference. Several patents have been filed for cold fusion schemes, and it would not be surprising if cold fusion becomes a commercial reality by the time this book is widely circulated. I confess to being caught up in cold fusion intrigue to the extent of actually taking delivery on several hundred ounces of palladium that were minted in cold fusion medallions. From a speculative standpoint, a commercially feasible cold fusion process could easily propel palladium prices over $1,000 an ounce. It seemed a reasonable gamble to hoard some of this metal—just in case.

I have followed cold fusion development since its inception. There is absolutely no question that some form of energy-producing process exists here. At the time of this writing, several applications were emerging. On the positive side, palladium appears to be the most efficient and consistent metal for generating a cold fusion reaction. On the negative side, several experiments seem to indicate that nickel can achieve the same type of positive energy production. Three approaches to cold fusion were touted as being of possible commercial scale in 1996. The first was the Pons/Fleischmann fusion in a jar using heavy water, a palladium cathode, and platinum wire. This device uses electrical current to begin the alleged fusion. Published results suggest that initial "reactors" will generate approximately 25 kilowatts to power a home or small building.

Strangely, one of the problems associated with initial cold fusion devices is the power conversion technology. Cold fusion generates heat. The heat must be harnessed to convert into electrical power. Thermal conversion is not an easy process at low temperatures. Unless cold fusion generates sufficient heat to convert into mechanical energy like a steam engine, equations for changing cold fusion into usable energy are extremely complex. Although skeptics have been turning the corner to accept this unusual phenomenon or "observation," the amount of positive energy has not been impressive. The palladium/platinum apparatus will require huge advancements before it finds its way into homes, vehicles, and power systems.

A second energy prospect is called *sono-luminescence.* You may be familiar with the unusual light that often appears in the wake of a powerboat at night. Sometimes the glow results from phosphorus algae. However, a blue hue associated with cavitation has been linked to a quasi-nuclear reaction that emits photons. Apparently, cavitation creates microscopic bubbles that collapse under extreme force. When these bubbles collapse, a photon is released as energy. There are experimental results that imply sono-luminescence can produce excess heat as a stand-alone process. When combined within a palladium shell or "target," cavitation seems to stimulate a cold fusion reaction. Still another approach is that of the Japanese, with palladium-based "energy generators" that rely on hydrogen. The assumption is that palladium has a subatomic matrix capable of absorbing hydrogen atoms and compressing them to form helium in extremely small reactions. In the Pons/Fleischmann approach, heavy water is the vehicle for transporting hydrogen into the palladium matrix. In theory, a pure hydrogen process could be more efficient and controllable. Laboratories in Russia, India, France, England, Germany, Japan, and the United States all report positive cold fusion findings. Although there is no definitive explanation for the apparent process, data and observations cannot be denied.

Cold fusion has enormous ecopolitical implications. Investors should recognize that the energy sector links to everything from transportation to environment control (heating and air conditioning) to all forms of manufacturing. Fossil fuels account for the enormous industrial infrastructure that is responsible for massive amounts of employment, capital investment, and revenue. Cold fusion could be the single most destructive economic force ever known if its introduction dislocates the conventional energy sector. In the past, most new technologies could be absorbed slowly. For example, nuclear energy has been gradually adopted because safety and cost issues have held back any formidable encroachment on the oil industry. Solar power does not share the same safety issues as conventional nuclear facilities, but efficiency and expense remained issues as of 1997. There are plans for wind farms, tidal generators, and even thermal power from volcanic activity. These new methods of powering society do not threaten to displace oil in a single sweep.

In contrast, cold fusion could provide an immediate transition from oil, coal, and gas to limitless clean energy. Why would such a transition present a problem? After all, isn't a power source like cold fusion our ultimate goal?

The problem is not in the process, but its implementation. Governments have been extremely reluctant to pursue cold fusion as a prospective science. The consensus is that cold fusion will come into use if it is real science. There is no incentive to hurry its commercial introduction because disbanding the fossil fuel machine is a daunting task for the private and public sectors. The billions invested in power plants and electricity delivery systems would be laid idle. The massive employment in the energy and related sectors would be rendered obsolete. Cars, trucks, planes, and trains would all require reevaluation and redesign. In a word, *upheaval* best describes the economic consequence of rapidly deployed cold fusion technology. Thus, the preferred timeline would be a slow move from experimental anomalies to small-scale laboratory curiosities. This appears to be the stage of cold fusion as of 1996. Thereafter, a modest commercial reactor might be tolerated if cold fusion exhibits no safety issues. This is the point of extreme investment interest. The moment a commercial cold fusion system is introduced, palladium could be the ultimate high flyer. Assuming cold fusion continues relying on palladium rather than nickel or some other process, the investment potential will be enormous. In fact, it may be impossible to obtain palladium once the rush begins.

Cold fusion is a trump card that may never be played. Even without this remarkable possibility, palladium has strong favorable fundamentals. Demand curves for autocatalysts, chemical processing, dental alloying, electronics/electrical, and even hoarding all look bright.

Autocatalysts

Although palladium's catalytic properties have been known for decades, it was not until the mid-1980s that experts noticed that this metal realized greater potential for pollution control in cars and trucks. Several developments were required to bring about palladium's success including the move away from tetraethyl lead as an octane enhancer and improved refining to remove sulfur from gasoline and diesel fuel. Palladium is highly sensitive to lead and sulfur contamination. Until these components were removed from fuels, it was virtually impossible to perfect a palladium device that could survive the required time for practical automotive and truck use.

Palladium is particularly effective in reducing unburned hydrocarbons. During cold starts, engines tend to burn rich fuel-to-air mixtures. By situating a palladium catalyst close to the initial exhaust, hydrocarbon emissions can be substantially decreased during the cold start phase and normal operation. As clean air becomes an increasing priority relative to population densities, the need for stricter tailpipe standards will intensify. This should translate into greater palladium demand. Figure 9–2 displays progress in autocatalyst use of palladium from 1986 forward.

Until 1989, most of the palladium used in autocatalysts was complementary to platinum. Once the palladium technology was perfected, demand assumed an extreme slope. As palladium use matures, the slope should fall off and more directly correlate with auto production. There were still many North American, European, and Japanese models that did not employ palladium technology in 1996. However, the ten- and fifteen-year projections call for demand equilibrium because expansion will be complete. This means that all car and truck models that can employ palladium eventually will.

The intriguing aspect of palladium's autocatalyst growth curve is its potential to exceed supplies unless price forces more moderate usage or mining keeps pace. With approximately 6.8 million ounces mined in 1996, there is a distinct possibility that autocatalysts will gobble up more than half the world's new annual supplies shortly into the twenty-first century. This paints an encouraging price picture. One moderating factor might be palladium recovery. Like platinum, palladium is not consumed in autocatalysts. Unlike platinum, palladium does not release as much recoverable supplies when used elsewhere.

Autocatalytic Use of Palladium 1986–96

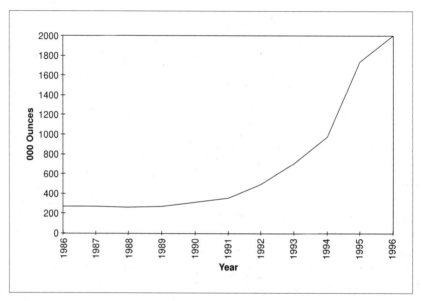

Electronic/Electrical

Palladium is extensively used in electronic components. Approximately 25 percent is for contacts, conductive pastes, specialized circuit components, and sensors. By far the largest electronic application is in manufacturing multilayer ceramic capacitors (MLCCs). Palladium has become an effective alternative to platinum-silver in MLCCs. These devices store electric charges like miniature batteries, discharging when needed. MLCCs are found in all forms of electronic components from personal computers to mobile phones and extremely precise mechanisms in military hardware. The growth in palladium consumption for MLCCs is directly related to expanding global electronics applications. Through the 1990s, there was a trade-off between surging MLCC use and advancing miniaturization technology. Palladium consumption was balanced between MLCC usage and the decreasing size per average unit. Research trends indicate MLCC circuits are approaching practical limits in miniaturization. Virtually every long-range forecast calls for accelerating growth in production and sales of electronics. Aside from the obvious pattern in Japan, North America, and Western Europe, entirely new communications infrastructures are being developed in South America, China, the Pacific Rim, India, and former Eastern Bloc countries.

In 1997, two communications technologies were under consideration for developing regions: wireless and fiber optic. Future wireless systems can consume more palladium because of the number of MLCCs needed in portable phones, beepers, and communications devices. However, my research indicates that hybrid systems are more probable and both fiber optics and wireless are evenly matched. Fiber optic systems require couplers and repeaters that use MLCCs. Switches and logic circuits for fiber optic systems use palladium plating and silver-palladium "tracks" on mission-critical printed circuit boards. Certainly, if China decided in favor of cellular or similar wireless communications systems, there might be a more favorable palladium outlook because of the sheer number of handheld units likely to be placed into operation. Figure 9–3 shows an impressive growth curve which should extend well into the next several decades.

If we combine the growth in production of electronics and autocatalysts alone, it is easy to project increasing supply pressures for palladium based on present production. I do not foresee any immediate substitutes for palladium in the electronics sector. MLCCs, hybrid integrated circuits, printed circuit boards, couplers, switches, and a host of related components will rely on palladium and platinum. Even as prices rise for these metals, better implementation can reduce required amounts in each component to a great extent. In my opinion, the electronic/electrical future for palladium remains bright.

Dental

Like gold, palladium is enjoying increasing popularity as dentistry moves away from silver-mercury amalgams. Palladium-gold alloys provide an excellent alternative to higher gold-content

F I G U R E   9–3

Electronic/Electrical Uses of Palladium

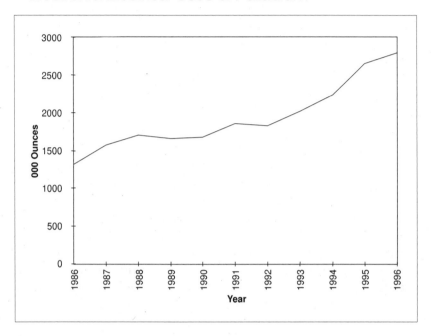

restorative materials in terms of price and durability. Restorative dentists point out that higher gold content is preferable when opposing surfaces involve a natural tooth against an inlay or onlay. However, if opposing surfaces are both restored material, the need for a "kinder" material is not as pressing. Palladium-gold material is harder and requires more careful "margin preparation." In Germany, where restorations are considered an art as well as a medical procedure, palladium is beginning to make a more positive impression. (No pun intended for those dentists out there!) The United States saw a pronounced increase in palladium-gold use from 1993 forward as a direct result of lower insurance payments for restorative procedures.

Demographics are likely to play an important role in rising dental demand through the year 2030. The leading edge of the post-World War II generation did not receive the full benefits of fluoridated water. The population age curve in the United States, Western Europe, and Japan indicates increasing restorative dental requirements will occur from the years 2000 forward to approximately 2025. Further, as Third World countries develop, there will be increasing demand for dental care. This can easily push the demand out beyond the year 2050. Figure 9–4 depicts the situation graphically.

There are a lot of teeth out there! However, earlier chapters mentioned the development of polymers and silicates that can be cast and implanted like their precious metal counterparts. If gold and palladium prices rise too high, there will be a push for nonmetal restorations. Judging by growth in autocatalysts and

F I G U R E   9–4

Use of Palladium in Dentistry

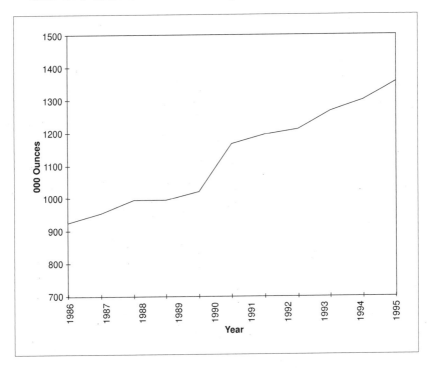

electronics, costly palladium is a distinct near-term possibility. Can the palladium price exceed that of gold? Given the more diversified strategic applications, investors could see palladium's value climb above gold's. Under such circumstances, expect a move back to more gold content in dental materials.

Chemical

Figure 9–5 projects demand for chemical applications. I previously covered the mainstays of this sector encompassing synthetic fiber manufacturing and hydrogen peroxide production.

Palladium demand for use in chemical processing has enjoyed a moderate growth that will continue as long as prices remain below approximately $280 per ounce. At prices above $300, alternative technologies become attractive. In particular,

F I G U R E 9–5

Chemical Uses of Palladium

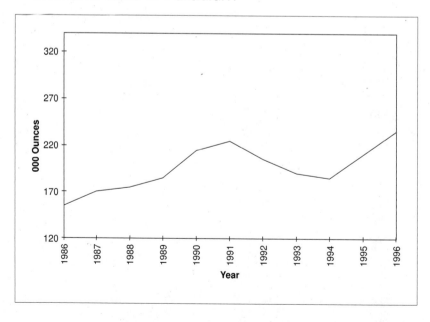

investors can expect different methods for producing industrial hydrogen peroxide or alternative bleaching technologies in paper manufacturing. I expect the chemical sector to be the first sacrificial lamb if palladium's other industrial demands push the price curve.

Palladium is also used to recover its platinum and rhodium sister metals. Systems using palladium "catch gauze" sacrifice palladium in return for platinum and, more specifically, rhodium. There is a question whether the chemical demand category has been a catchall for increasing amounts of palladium used in cold fusion experimentation. Rumors for cold fusion reached as high as 50,000 ounces in 1996. This is a significant amount because it would account for nearly all the growth in the chemical sector from 1994 forward. However, industry representatives strongly refute any cold fusion use above "nominal levels" of a few thousand ounces.

The synthetic fiber industry and paper manufacturing industry are highly cost-sensitive. Both involve large volume and low selling prices. This means chemical palladium use is likely to become more reactive to higher palladium prices. Based on the ratio of usage, I do not believe chemical applications will decisively swing toward palladium. Because it is only marginal, chemical consumption could sharpen a price movement based on changes in supply or autocatalyst and electronic sector consumption.

Analysis of the paper and fiber industries shows steady growth related to increasing global wealth and demand. There has been a sharp increase in paper shipments to the CIS and former Eastern Bloc countries which has been attributed to more freedom in the press and rising print media advertising. Commercial enterprise in China is also increasing that nation's paper consumption. In fact, the United States is one of the largest importers of Chinese printing, which can be highly competitive even with additional shipping costs. Industrialized nations have been careful to impose a sense of environmental responsibility on emerging economies. This is why environmentally friendly paper bleaching is likely to be the process of choice.

Clothing is certainly a growth industry. Global capacity for natural fibers like cotton and wool is limited by the practical growing regions and cycles. This points to greater use of synthetic materials and, consequently, greater demand for palladium in the manufacturing of purified terephthalic acid.

Jewelry

Palladium is exclusively used for alloying platinum and gold. As a precious metal, palladium has gained popularity over nickel and other metals. The trend toward using between 5 percent and 15 percent palladium content in platinum jewelry slowed during the late 1990s because most platinum jewelry was consumed in Japan where the status of "pure" platinum discouraged purchasing alloyed pieces. However, Italy began increasing palladium use for producing high-karat white gold. Palladium alloying produces a more workable product with better color than a nickel counterpart. The trade-off is the significantly higher price of palladium compared with nickel. Inexpensive gold chain rarely uses palladium. Some Middle East manufacturers have moved into platinum jewelry for export to Japan and some local consumption. Figure 9–6 graphs palladium consumption for jewelry from 1986 through 1996.

As this graph illustrates, jewelry consumption is at approximately the same level and configuration as chemical usage. Together, these categories will probably be more price-sensitive than other uses because it is easier to substitute other metals for jewelry applications and change bleaching agents in paper mills.

Other Demand

Palladium's sensitivity to sulfur has generated applications for the metal as a "scrubbing element" whereby a palladium catalyst is used to remove trace amounts of sulfur from fuels like diesel and kerosene. Palladium is also used to reduce aromatics that form noxious fumes when burned. Like platinum and rhodium, palladium has properties that are suited for oxygen sensors. Palladium is used for anticorrosion plating in chemical process plants. Finally, a limited amount of palladium is used for investment bars, coins, and medallions.

F I G U R E   9–6

Use of Palladium in Jewelry 1986–96

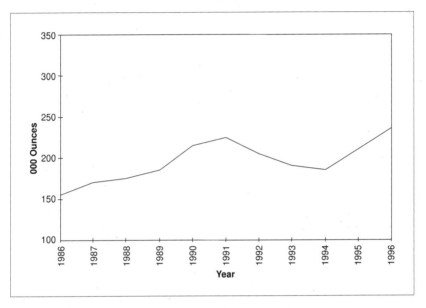

Palladium hoarding has been too insignificant to justify its own usage category. However, this may change as the metal's popularity increases. The central problem with investing in physical palladium is its lack of supply. Although more wealthy individuals may afford delivery of a 100-ounce futures contract, this is beyond the means of the majority of investors. Aside from cost, housing 100-ounce bars represents a storage problem and risk. Russia minted a "Ballerina" coin that is used as a physical investment vehicle. Unfortunately, the coin is an alloy and is not as desirable as the pure bars and certified medallions that have a 0.9995 fine content. Johnson Matthey produces one-ounce bars in small quantities, and it has been difficult to find dealers with inventory.

Shortly after the March 1989 cold fusion press conference, a series of palladium medallions were marketed. The most common were the half-ounce and full-ounce "cold fusion medallions" sold by Benchmark Commemoratives from New Hampshire. These pieces had 0.9998 content and were individually numbered for tracking. Approximately 15,000 ounces were minted by various companies hoping to cash in on a cold fusion frenzy. The small quantity of medallions has made them more valuable as collectors' items than for metal content.

Japanese hoarding was estimated at approximately 20,000 ounces in 1996. This was the same for 1995 and 1994. Overall, investment demand is a matter of education. As long as palladium is overshadowed by platinum and has very limited jewelry use, cash investment will be static.

The total demand picture appears quite positive. Figure 9–7 plots all major use categories as a total. The slope toward the end of the 1990s was rising, and most fundamental indications point to the same pattern through several decades into the next millenium.

F I G U R E 9–7

Total Palladium Usage

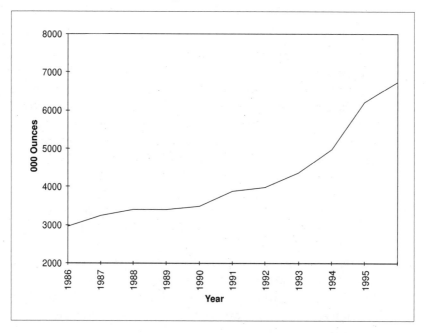

As you will see from the discussion of supply, palladium has been on a hand-to-mouth basis for a long time. It is not easy to develop new palladium production. This metal is extremely rare and presents many challenges.

SUPPLY

Palladium is a counterpart of platinum. Thus, most of the supply coverage for platinum applies to palladium as well. The largest producer has been Russia, followed by South Africa, North America, and others. Figure 9–8 shows producer positions as of 1996.

Russian mine output is the same as platinum with the majority coming as a by-product of Norril'sk Nickel. There have been some palladium-specific developments in some CIS regions; how-

F I G U R E   9–8

Palladium Supply by Region

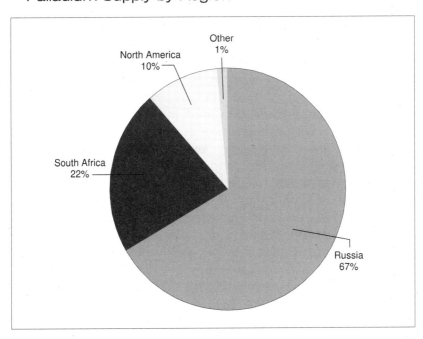

ever, these properties are not expected to add appreciable supplies until well beyond the year 2020.

South African supplies will track the same course as platinum with almost identical mine development. Although some areas have more palladium-rich ore, expect the emphasis to remain with platinum and gold unless palladium prices move above $280.

By 1997 the two regions with the most potential for boosting palladium supplies were North America and Indonesia. Both Canada and the United States had significant palladium mine developments as mentioned in Chapter 8. North American Palladium in Canada represented a beginning with estimated annual capacity of 7,000 tons of ore per day by 1997. Several million ounces in reserves are located in the Ile de Lac region where the mine is located. Originally, analysis indicated that ore yielded 95 percent palladium with only 5 percent in other metals. Ratios have changed in favor of more platinum and gold with about an 85 percent to 15 percent yield.

Firm prices with good prospects encouraged the rebuilding and capacity expansion for the Stillwater mine in Nevada. Along with North American Palladium, projections call for output exceeding 200,000 ounces per year through 1998. Milling could grow capacity to more than 500,000 ounces per year which could elevate North America to be the number two producing region.

Will wonders never cease? Kalimantan, Indonesia, may represent the most impressive new gold and mineral fields ever discovered. Along with gold reserves that may range from 50 to 150 million ounces, ore analysis reveals potential for palladium production exceeding 1 million ounces per year. Depending on the speed of development, full capacity should be available by 2005. Of course, we cannot be sure about the scope of "full capacity." During the 1950s, geologists believed South African accessible reserves would be depleted within ten years . . . . "Fooled ya!"

The Pacific Rim represents vast unexplored geological riches. I believe investors can easily see a 400 percent increase in palladium supplies by 2010 and a 100 percent increase each decade thereafter. Figure 9–9 breaks out production from 1986 through 1996.

F I G U R E   9–9

Palladium Supply by Region 1986–96

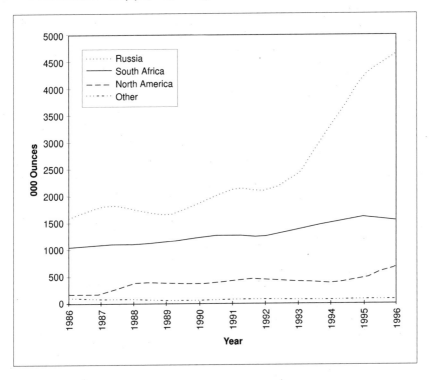

As with any analysis based on shifting sands, Figure 9–9 does not paint a realistic picture moving forward from 1996 because it fails to consider explosive growth potential in the "other" regions. Australia, Indonesia, China, Chile, Peru, and a host of other promising regions combine to make this category as impressive as Russia or South Africa. One projection based on properties cataloged toward the end of 1996 provides the forecast for new-region production illustrated in Figure 9–10.

As the chart reveals, new regions are forecast to rival South Africa. If history is our guide, this projection is understated. In the late 1980s, gold production was thought to be at a peak. Not long ago, the Earth was believed to be flat!

F I G U R E   9–10

Projected Production of Palladium for New Regions

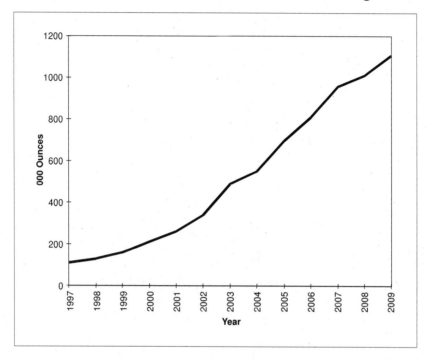

Figure 9–11 plots supply and demand to provide a perspective from 1986 forward. The balance is almost uncanny, with a near match from 1986 forward. Interestingly, projections for both supply and demand show the same close proximity for each curve. This is extremely important for the price dynamic. As with platinum, any supply disruption can immediately send palladium spiraling to new highs. This was the case in 1997 when Russia suddenly stopped palladium and platinum shipments. As previously mentioned in Chapter 8, prices immediately reacted higher. Palladium touched $210 per ounce from its interim consolidation near $150. This 40 percent price spectacular proves how exciting and potentially rewarding palladium trading can be!

F I G U R E 9–11

Palladium Supply versus Demand 1986–96

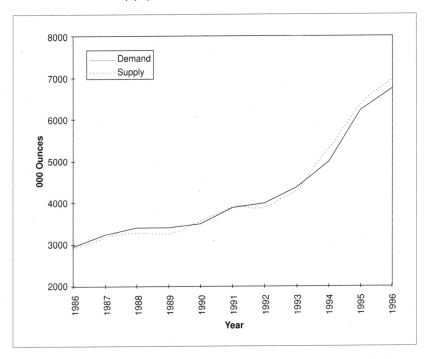

CONCLUSION

It should be apparent that platinum group metals (PGMs) offer excellent long-term potential for price appreciation. Although computerized vehicle pollution control systems threaten to obviate autocatalysts to an extent, I do not foresee a significant decline in the use of converters well into the twenty-first century. The mandate for "zero emissions" in California and New York will turn attention to alternative transportation, which may include commercially feasible electric cars and trucks. Again, such prospects extend well into the twenty-first century.

Unlike silver, PGMs have a strong industrial foundation because available amounts are substantially smaller and technological alternatives less prominent. Digital photography can easily assume the premier role in taking snapshots and newsprint pictures, sharply decreasing demand for silver. No such decline in palladium use looms close on the horizon.

Palladium also offers unique opportunities for the stock investor because there are publicly traded primary palladium mines like North American Palladium (on NASD small cap) and investors can participate in entities controlling the Stillwater mine. I expect to see more palladium companies as the popularity and necessity of this metal continue to grow. Palladium may not have the luster and visual appeal of gold or its long-standing reverence. However, in a modern industrial society, palladium can do better than gold.

CHAPTER 10

Investing in Stocks

Although a less direct means of acquiring precious metals, one of the most popular ways to participate is through stocks of producing companies. It is not the purpose of this book to recommend specific stocks by naming particular companies that are "good buys." By the time any book goes to press and is digested, corporate structures can change as can the economic environment. However, certain fundamentals should remain in place as long as precious metals markets remain open and free. Efficient producers will have good equity performance. The evaluation of precious metals companies requires the same attention as does an examination of a food, computer, or drug producer. What is the product? Does the company exclusively produce gold, silver, or platinum group metals? Are precious metals coincidental to the production of other base metals? How is the product positioned? Who manages the company and what is his or her management style? What are costs relative to revenues? What are prospects for profit margins?

Because most of this book is dedicated to evaluating metals as products, there is no need for repetition. However, there are subtle areas worth exploring. For example, how are gold, silver, platinum, and palladium marketed? We have identified various uses, but is there an active effort to "sell" precious metals? Then, we should touch on cost structures. Can we define cost for an ounce of gold or silver? Finally, we should look at capital structures that reveal the price of entering the precious metals business and the attractiveness of mergers and acquisitions. Will investors see a trend toward new mining companies or a move to consolidate? Through the 1990s, several large mining companies went into "merger mania." The economics of mining forced alliances between former competitors. Politics played an increasing role in securing mineral rights in foreign territories. All these developments influence stock performance.

MARKETING

Precious metals are promoted by trade groups, retailers, and governments more than by individual producing companies. It is rare to see an advertisement by a mining company touting virtues of gold, silver, or platinum group metals. Instead, ads and marketing campaigns are placed by the World Gold Council, the Gold Institute, the United States Treasury, government mints, coin and bullion dealers, and jewelry manufacturers. Producing companies may conduct image campaigns to promote stock values; however, the product is not the focal point. Investors should examine marketing efforts as a whole against specific corporate positions to determine whether a stock represents a good value.

Throughout the years, various trade groups have marketed precious metals based on traditional perceptions. If you read research reports from these institutions, you will see a heavy bias toward projecting higher prices. Regardless of reality, trade groups are supposed to be optimistic. In the precious metals area, "up" is an essential attitude. The World Gold Council and similar organizations receive funding from members who are producers. Marketing strategies center around "telling the story" of why precious metals are good investments. When economic environments favor metals, there is a tendency to see more advertising and marketing. Spokespeople frequently appear on television and radio programs to paint positive pictures. As an adjunct activity, public relations efforts reach out to the stock brokerage community to make sure precious metals companies are properly represented.

Monitoring these marketing activities is important. There is a correlation between efforts made by trade groups and the acceptance of their members' stock offerings. When the senior metals analyst of Prudential Bache is convinced that silver is a good investment, customers flock to futures, options, individual stocks, and precious metals mutual funds. This additional demand can translate into better near-term performance. By the same logic, if perception is negative, investors will seek alternatives more aggressively. Most prospective investors have seen advertising for silver, gold, and platinum. Small ads appear in *The Wall Street Journal* and *Investors Business Daily* offering one-ounce coins and even five-pound blocks of silver. This marketing helps maintain a steady interest in metal at the retail investment level. Jewelry marketing is equally important for promoting retail sales volume. Consider the amount of metal consumed by the jewelry sector. The more popular jewelry with high metal content becomes, the better prices will be supported.

Investors do not always make the connection between a Rolex watch advertisement and gold or platinum values. Yet, a strong influence exists. Ads for solid 18-karat gold Rolex watches market large quantities of gold. Sears, J. C. Penny, Wal-Mart, Consumers Distributors, and host of other chain stores can move significant quantities of gold chain, pendants, earrings, rings, bangles, lockets, silver jewelry, and watches. When these retail giants run jewelry "specials" they become marketing arms for mining companies.

Occasionally, the World Gold Council or Silver Institute will run advertising. However, these trade associations provide more fundamental marketing in the form of brochures, informative pamphlets, and research reports. In fact, this book contains information derived from these excellent sources. During inflationary periods, trade associations and groups help to keep precious metals in the limelight. During times of monetary stability, the concentration is on maintaining awareness about the virtues of precious metals.

The truly exemplary performance of gold mining stocks and mutual funds during most of the 1990s changed some marketing philosophies. Companies realized the investment trend was too strongly entrenched in paper asset accumulation. This made it practical to market the precious metals "business" as much as the products. Many mining companies hired public relations firms to address issues like environmental concerns, job growth, economic contributions to communities, and profitability. The mining community seized the opportunity to market its business and attract investors, fund managers, and financial consultants.

COST STRUCTURES

A curious phenomenon took place from 1987 forward. Just after the October 1987 "Black Monday" crash, gold stocks began leading industry performances. Yet, interest in gold was static moving through the 1990s. Why would gold stocks move higher while gold was unable to break out of a moderate trading range? A combination of excellent marketing and increasing operational efficiency provides the answer. The average world price for extracting an ounce of gold was declining. Figure 10–1 provides a graph of estimated extraction costs projected through the year 2000.

The slope of the cost decline is likely to flatten and may even begin rising into the next few decades. Yet, the decline in cost helps to explain how a gold company can perform well even as prices decline. The decrease in costs was so dramatic that it actually offset any price weakness. This same situation held true for silver and, to a less extent, the platinum group metals. In the case of platinum and palladium, recovery from old catalysts and components accounted for a decrease in average prices while mining costs remained relatively firm. Silver production was estimated to cost between $0.50 per ounce to approximately $5. The Mackay School of Mines, University of Nevada, released a 1995 report entitled "The U.S. Gold Industry 1994," which analyzed 1994 cash costs for U.S. gold mines in terms of:

Extraction	$107
Processing	84
Administration	18
Royalties	14
Taxes	9
Total	$232

This was an average estimate and carried projections for reductions in extraction costs because of increasing efficiency. A trend toward lower cost was aided by lower interest rates and computerized administrative operations. In 1994, eleven mines had estimated operating costs below $200 per ounce, whereas thirty-eight mines were less than $300. Compare these costs to an average price that exceeded $360 per ounce.

F I G U R E 10–1

Average World Gold Cost

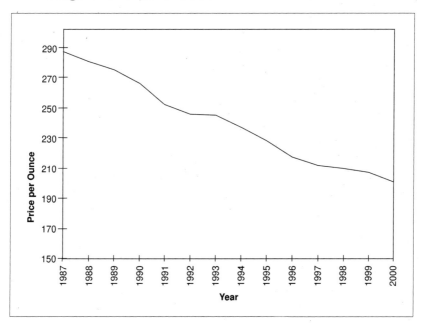

As long as technology pushes the efficiency envelope forward, we should expect healthy stock performance. Gold stocks, in particular, offer a double-edged protection and appreciation incentive. First, gold production is profitable. Then, the "product" offers the ultimate hedge against a monetary meltdown. This combination makes gold stocks and mutual funds fundamentally attractive. Because other precious metals are associated with gold production, there is some participation for silver and the platinum group. However, most of the stock emphasis has been on gold. It is important to recognize that costs for gold are not always directly correlated with silver, platinum, and palladium. Precious metals that come from primary copper, nickel, lead, tin, and zinc have significantly different cost allocations.

Suppose you are considering investing in stocks. When you conduct your research, try to determine how costs are allocated. What is the "cost per ounce" and how does it compare with alternatives? As previously mentioned, mines come in many configurations. From deep-shaft properties that have dominated in South Africa to surface mines like those in South Carolina, costs will be substantially different. If you are inclined to maintain a "dynamic" portfolio to seek maximum performance, then monitoring cost structures will be extremely important. Keep track of each property acquisition and type. It is also important to associate base and precious metal production. Make sure you evaluate nickel, copper, and other mines in conjunction with companies that are exclusively focused on gold, silver, or the platinum group.

It is often difficult to determine which metals lead profit margins. For example, when copper has a cost of $0.50 per pound and a selling price of $1.20, it is easy to understand why by-product silver might be sacrificed. If silver is at $30 per ounce, copper might become secondary to extracting precious metals. Demand stability for base metals' prospective growth indicates precious metals will remain the by-product through the foreseeable future. Therefore, you should concentrate on overall efficiency rather than allocations for precious metals. Keep an eye on political changes that might affect royalty rates and taxes. Never forget that governments are always the partner in any business, especially mining.

Certainly, mutual fund managers are involved in cost analysis for the precious and base metals industries. This makes mutual fund investment efficient and, perhaps, less risky. There are hundreds of cost factors to consider when you evaluate individual stocks. For most of us, there is neither enough time nor resources to conduct as complete a research job as do professional managers. Still, the exercise is often fun and worth the effort for those inclined to "go it alone."

CAPITAL STRUCTURE

Mining is generally an expensive business. Capital investment has been a barrier to new entries in modern mining companies. However, there have been exciting discoveries and stock issues that prove there is still room for new players. Two categories warrant special attention. Established companies with proven reserves and track records make up the industry's foundation. Small exploration and development companies provide a second tier. Nothing illustrates market potential and danger as much as the 1995–96 introduction of Bre-X. This Canadian upstart managed to hype a property with initial estimated reserves exceeding 70 million ounces of gold. Politics and capital structure forced Bre-X into a joint venture with Freeport-McMoran. With more intrigue than a modern spy thriller or action movie, Bre-X unfolded into one of the greatest scams in modern stock market history. Once the alignment with Freeport-McMoran took place, new surveys revealed almost no gold in the Bre-X property. Millions in stock value evaporated in an instant.

When the Bre-X "find" was initially announced in 1996, I appeared on CNBC to comment on its potential impact on gold prices. In my brief five-minute appearance, I concentrated on two points. First, I was skeptical about the huge reserve estimates because my research indicated that several reputable mining companies had been exploring the area with far less spectacular results. Thus, caution was in order. Then I said gold prices would not be significantly affected because production would not be immediate. On both counts, I was correct.

You might have come to the same conclusion. With just a small amount of research, the Bre-X situation would have seemed questionable. Frankly, I was at a loss to understand how so many experts bought into the Bre-X story.

Small start-up companies can give investors an exciting ride, but you must always be careful. A Bre-X situation is not likely to become the rule; it is the exception. Be wary of sensational stories about discoveries and gold-laden properties. For example, my own investigation suggests some of the projections for Bre-X and similarly situated companies have been overstated. That's marketing! If it were so easy to find gold, the metal would be worthless, or certainly worth less! On the other hand, new companies can yield exceptional profits if they are in the right place at the right time with the correct incentives and ethics. Investing in the stock of small start-up companies is serious business. All too often, we take promotional literature at face value. Here is a checklist to follow if you are solicited for such an investment:

- Take the time and make the effort to check with authorities about the company being offered and the brokerage firm making the offer. Never make an investment commitment by telephone unless you have had an opportunity to review facts and verify sources.
- Consider the nature of the offering. Where is the company located? Is it incorporated in the United States, Canada, or within a member nation of the European Union? If it is a South American or African company, make sure it is properly registered with authorities. Ask for geological surveys and assessments. If none are available, it is a red flag!
- New discoveries are likely to be in undeveloped regions. Consider political environments. How stable is the government? Is the company well connected?
- Be practical in your commitment. Never overextend and always view investments in small or start-up companies as speculative. Never put day-to-day living capital on the line; invest only your risk capital.

If you follow these four instructions, you should eliminate some of the exposure associated with new companies and stock issues. No checklist is perfect. Even well-established companies stumble and fall.

Toward the end of the 1990s there was a series of mergers and acquisitions among the large mining companies. Most notable was the four-way "Pac-man" involving Barrick Gold, Placer Dome, Homestake, and Santa Fe Pacific Gold. This marked the continuation of a powerful industry trend toward capital consolidation. Whether this extends or dissipates remains a question for the future. But no company is beyond merging or being acquired. Such consolidations represent enormous profit opportunities. Properties, technology, and capital can combine to double and triple values, or even multiply them by greater amounts. In 1996 I recommended a portfolio consisting of a highly diversified entities. In the United States there was:

Newmont
Homestake
Freeport-McMoRan
Santa Fe Pacific
Royal Gold (small cap)

In Canada the firms were:

Barrik Gold
Placer Dome
Noranda
Lac Minerals
BP Minerals

In South Africa I recommended:

Anglo American
GFSA
Gencor
JCI
Randgold

In Australia, the following were recommended:

Normandy Poseidon
North Limited
Goldfields
Plutonic Resources

These were primarily gold-producing companies. I mentioned North American Palladium, Chevron Resources, and Engelhard for palladium. As stock markets in Chile, Peru, and Russia gain stability, I expect excellent equity opportunities. For simplicity, you might consider mutual funds specializing in "emerging" foreign mining companies.

The facts clearly show a new precious metals bonanza was on the horizon through the 1980s and 1990s. Despite the lack of rising prices, profitability expanded along with incentives to improve technology and increase properties. The trend remained incredibly strong for virtually all precious metals except, perhaps, silver. This is not to say prospects for silver discouraged production; simply, primary silver mining was limited to countries like Chile, Mexico, and Peru. Even silver properties in these countries were tenuous because of the volatility associated with base metal counterparts. Although this text did not examine copper, lead, tin, zinc, and other base metal mining operations, these metals have exhibited exhilarating trends of their own. Volatility in base metals can translate into good or bad stock performance. Generally, metals are considered economically sensitive. A booming consumer economy demands greater amounts of base metals. Weak economies slow consumption in housing, transportation, electronics, and packaging. Just as recycling impacts platinum and palladium, it can take a toll on metals like aluminum and tin. Recycled aluminum from cans costs a fraction of the virgin metal. The efficiency of collecting and recycling placed the entire industry into near crisis because prices could not support primary production.

Thus, the metals industry is extremely dynamic and interwoven. This suggests any approach to equity investment should follow basic rules that apply to all industry groups. I believe an expanding world economy translates into profit potential. While there are bound to be bumps in the road, metal is here to stay. Mining, processing, and marketing companies should perform well in stock portfolios.

Projections

$\mathbf{A}$ny long-term forecast is simply a conjuration of "best guesses" based on current facts. If there is anything constant about precious metals markets, it is their propensity for dramatic and fundamental change. Precious metals are emotional investments. Value is based on a dual standard rooted in rarity and utility. This book has attempted to separate fact from desire to provide an objective view of the four most popular investment metals. This is an important endeavor because of the tendency to romanticize these markets and to lose reasonable objectivity. My personal experience spans the prohibition of U.S. gold ownership only through its emancipation in 1975. I am not a product of the Great Depression nor have I had the pleasure of gold coinage in my pocket (yet). My exposure to the first half of the twentieth century is based on discussions with those who were there and my review of associated documentation. For whatever their value, I became aware of precious metals during the transition from asset-backed currency to floating exchange. Having seen how the structure of precious metals markets can change, I must be cautious about offering predictions.

Indeed, the historical perspective on which investors might rely is brief. Gold and silver have only recently become commodities without monetary ties. Platinum and palladium were just coming of age in the late 1970s. Everything from how people use precious metals to investors' very perception has been challenged. Production technology has advanced as well as exploration techniques. Vast new territories are opening. New government structures are forming. Global communication is expanding and wealth accumulation is no longer restricted to post-World War II industrialized nations.

All these changes are bound to impact precious metals. The ultimate question is, "How?" As bold as any prediction might seem, I believe there is a pattern. The pivotal event that converted gold into money was supply expansion during the Mercantile period. When sufficient gold could be circulated, it assumed a place along with silver as nations' monetary foundations. Once world economies expanded more rapidly than gold and silver supplies, the monetary link had to be broken.

Humanity has endured the Stone Age, Bronze Age, Middle Ages, Mercantilism, the Industrial Revolution, rapid transit, the Communication Age, the Electronic Revolution, and the Information Age. Each represented a structural change that broke old rules and formed new guidelines. With the Information Age, there is a global awareness of modern society, politics, products, and services. It is as easy for a student in China to observe the latest toys in the Sharper Image catalogue as it is for the customer in New York City or Chicago. The Internet takes us well beyond the Communication Age represented by telephone, television, and radio. We are exchanging and processing information, conducting transactions, and monitoring the world. At the same time, technology is altering living standards almost daily.

Although I have discouraged the idea of returning to a gold standard, I offer these snippet observations to provide a ray of hope to die-hard gold and silver "bugs." It's possible we will return to some form of hard asset monetary standard. Consider trends toward consolidation. We see consolidation of currencies and markets. We see consolidation through corporate mergers and acquisitions. We see political consolidation. At some stage, the easiest way to consolidate monetary systems is to pick a standard. The standard will be defined by a world community consisting of government organizations subject to human tendencies. While the "Group of 5" or "Group of 7" may have dictated monetary relationships, such control has historically been temporary. What is the possibility the world will return to gold or silver to establish values and parity?

CHANCES OF PRECIOUS METALS AS FUTURE RESERVES

If the rate of silver and gold production begins to substantially exceed consumption, I believe there may be strong incentives to return to fixed standards. There will be issues of trust as the Third World industrializes. There will be concerns about cyber transactions and computerized bank accounts. Although there are predictions for a violent return to gold and silver in the form of a paper crash, I am not sure this must be the form of transition. The amazing tool for disseminating information over the Internet and by television can be used to reintroduce silver coinage and gold-backed transactions. Just as the closing of the Gold Window did not bring disaster, the reopening of negotiated gold or silver instruments should not upset the system.

Why would we return to gold or silver? In the absence of monetary panic, a metals standard must be convenient. If gold and silver become cheap, they can be as convenient as alternative metals and paper currencies. If inventories can be logged and tracked electronically, hard assets offer a measure of security that becomes convenient because fear is not healthy for active world markets.

Trends in supply and demand reviewed in this book suggest silver and gold are on track for the same expansion seen during the original Gold Rush. Massive amounts of new metal may become available and a market must be developed if the industry is to survive. The most stable market is monetary absorption. Demographics allow alternatives. There is always a chance cultural demand from China, India, and the Pacific Rim will match supply. If this develops, monetary applications may be held in check.

Without new demand, I do not see effective ways to offset the progress of digital photography against silver halide film or the sizable expansion in world gold output. Even with outside projections for electronics, thermal and reflective treatments, chemical processes, and other industrial applications, the equations do not seem to favor bull markets.

If metals are monetized, speculative roles will diminish. However, mining stocks can become as solid as utilities. Once value parity is properly established, producers will have assured markets with absolute profit margins. Thereafter, volume and efficiency will distinguish between the better and less desirable companies. Systems for storing and tracking metal will be needed. Where there is a need, there is an investment opportunity. All businesses related to precious metals will derive some benefit from the stability of monetary roles. This means that there will still be opportunities for gain. The approach will be different.

It is difficult to predict whether nations will see central banks divest before any new standard is established or whether "reserve assets" will be held as an insurance policy. As long as there are treasury hoards, there will be a monetary relationship with the stored metal. Sometimes you have to temporarily give up a relationship to save a marriage. Perhaps this will be the next chapter in the dynamic life of silver and gold.

Certainly, the formation of unified markets in Europe, the Americas, and the Far East began a process of gold divestiture marked by central bank sales from Portugal and Belgium to Australia. The 1997 price depression that overwhelmed gold and silver was aided by pronouncements that metal was being converted into money. Both the sale of Australian gold and the potential of revaluing German reserves as a monetary ploy demonstrated the continuation of gold's role as a monetary instrument.

I would not be surprised if a massive reallocation of central bank reserves takes place before hints of a new monetary role surface. Money must circulate. When gold is in central bank vaults, it cannot act as money. With metal discoveries in virtually every corner on Earth, I am optimistic that we can reestablish bonds with precious metals without economic dislocation. In other words, nations that have in-ground reserves will not necessarily dominate as economic powerhouses. Instead, we will see a smooth flow of new metal to market in conjunction with diversified exchanges of previously existing supplies.

FUTURE USES IN INDUSTRY

Platinum and palladium are likely to march to different drummers. Prospects for expanding industrial applications seem encouraging. Even if there is a move away from autocatalysts, there appear to be enough new applications to fill any consumption void. I like to dream. The possibility of platinum fuel cells or palladium cold fusion reactions is sufficient incentive for me to accumulate a quantity of these metals. No, I am not inclined to bet the farm. It is not necessarily a good idea to store a thousand ounces under your bed or even in an expensive safe deposit box. A small collection can ride the wave if exciting new technologies develop.

The electronic explosion will be a massive force driving the demand side of precious metals. I cannot speak about the next developments in electroactive polymers and any potential to encroach on silver, gold, platinum, or palladium. By 1997, there were still no viable replacements for metals in electronic components. I believe there is a consensus that electronics are a growth sector that will take precious metals along for a strong demand ride. Demographics suggest untapped demand is enormous. Wealth patterns confirm demographics.

So there may never be a return to metal as a monetary standard, but it may never matter. Gold, silver, platinum, and palladium are still on a technological fast track for industrial usage.

A true follower of precious metals must study geology, technology, geography, demographic patterns, politics, economics, and history. Gold, silver, platinum, and palladium can take you down fascinating roads. Read about cutting edge science and all four metals are there. Pick up any electronic device and most will be within the components. Observe the open Middle East markets—gold is there. People's lives have been, and will continue to be, surrounded and influenced by precious metals. I encourage you to read more, study more—and perhaps buy more, just in case. However, always try to be objective and avoid the spell precious metals can often cast!

APPENDIX

UNITS OF MEASURE

Factors

20 pennyweights = 1 ounce
12 ounces = 1 pound
1 ordinary ounce = 0.9155 troy ounces
1 ordinary pound = 14.58 troy ounces
1 troy ounce = 31.103 grams = 480 grains
1 troy ounce = 0.0311033 kilogram
1 troy pound = 0.37224 kilogram
1 kilogram = 32.1507 troy ounces
1 tonne = 32,151 troy ounces
karat = gold purity in parts per 24
100% pure = 24 karat = 1000 fine
91.7% pure = 22 karat = 917 fine
75% pure = 18 karat = 750 fine
58.5% pure = 14 karat = 585 fine
41.6% pure = 10 karat = 416 fine

Avoirdupois Weights and Conversions

27 11/32 grains = 1 dram
16 drams = 1 ounce
16 ounces = 1 pound
1 pound = 7,000 grains
14 pounds = 1 stone (British)
100 pounds = 1 hundredweight (U.S.)
112 pounds = 8 stone = 1 hundredweight (British)
2,000 pounds = 1 short ton (U.S. ton)

2,240 pounds = 1 long ton (British ton)
160 stone = 1 long ton
20 hundredweight = 1 ton
1 pound = 0.4536 kilogram
1 hundredweight (cwt.) = 45.359 kilograms
1 short ton = 907.18 kilograms
1 long ton = 1,016.05 kilograms

Metric Weights and Conversions

1,000 grams = 1 kilogram
100 kilograms = 1 quintal
1 tonne = 1,000 kilograms = 10 quintals
1 kilogram = 2.240622 pounds
1 quintal = 220.462 pounds
1 tonne = 2204.6 pounds
1 tonne = 1.102 short tons
1 tonne = 0.9842 long ton

INDEX